A FIELD GUIDE TO
MONSTERS

HYLAS
PUBLISHING

Hylas Publishing

First Published in 2004 by Hylas Publishing
129 Main Street, Irvington, New York, 10533

Publisher: Sean Moore
Creative Director: Karen Prince
Art Director: Gus Yoo
Editorial Director: Gail Greiner
Designers: Shamona Stokes, Pak Rojanapisit
Editors: Hannah Choi, Angda Goel
Proofreader: Ginger Skinner

First American Edition published in 2004
08 09 10 11 10 9 8 7 6 5 4 3

ISBN: 1-59258-088-2

Printed and bound in China.

www.hylaspublishing.com

A FIELD GUIDE TO
MONSTERS

Dave Elliott · C.J. Henderson · R. Allen Leider

HYLAS
PUBLISHING

TABLE OF CONTENTS

INTRODUCTION

Though no one can fully take the place of Professor Abraham Van Helsing, with this new edition of *A Field Guide to Monsters*, we have aspired to continue with the cause that the good Professor single-handedly pioneered during the nineteenth century—monster eradication from the Earth. Some may call us modern-day heroes, if they so insist, but we are only doing what we believe with our hearts is vital to the survival of mankind as we know it.

Much of the present population seem to be content living in denial about the existence of monsters. However, with this book, we hope to not only raise awareness about monsters, but also reintroduce Van Helsing's life story and work to the world.

Professor Abraham Van Helsing was always a man of action. Born in the Netherlands and educated at the University of Rotterdam, he had set his hopes on becoming a medical doctor. But during his final semester, his close friend, Peter Hopkins, was stricken with a rare blood disorder. Reported stories of the time say that Hopkins had died but then had come back to life. A record of Hopkins' subsequent death can be found in the archives of the local newspaper, which published an all-too-brief account of the tragedy. After his friend's death, Van Helsing decided to forego his career as a general practitioner in order to specialize in the study of obscure blood diseases.

The Professor traveled much over the next forty years, studying blood disorders around the world. However, it was one adventure in particular, taking him from England to the heart of Transylvania, that moved the Professor to write down his findings on paper.

In 1890, the Professor met Bram Stoker, who, at the time, was the manager of the Lyceum Theatre. Stoker became obsessed with Van Helsing's stories and started to write down accounts of his adventures. It was then that Van Helsing asked Stoker to help him on a nonfiction work—a field guide to the monsters he had come across on his travels, which would specifically focus on the vampire.

One day, three years later, Van Helsing was urgently called to London. There had been a sighting of a vampire. But not just any vampire—this was Dracula, king of the blood-drinking beasts. Van Helsing hoped that if Dracula were destroyed, then all of his subordinates would also cease to be. This proved to be mere wishful thinking on Van Helsing's part.

The Professor's epic battles with Dracula fascinated Stoker and he transcribed the entire story with the advantage of being able to interview any relevant witnesses—survivors, family members, and any of Dracula's living victims who may have narrowly escaped eternal blood thirst. Stoker even had access to the Professor's journals and diaries.

Van Helsing had assumed that all of this effort was going into his field guide. By the time he realized the cruel truth—that Stoker was writing for personal fame, and not for the salvation of mankind—it was too late. Bram Stoker's novel *Dracula* sold out like wildfire. Translated into multiple languages, it spread around the globe immediately. Van Helsing never spoke to Stoker again and tore up every royalty check that the writer sent him.

In private, Van Helsing condemned Stoker for dooming mankind, for he foresaw that once vampires were trivialized as a work of fiction, the incredible threat that they posed on humanity would never be taken seriously. He was proved right when a year after the publication of *Dracula*, Van Helsing published his own *Field Guide to Monsters* in 1898. The book sold well, but was treated as a work of parody and his book tour appearances were always drowned out by laughter from the audience. *Dracula* had done its damage.

The tour came to an abrupt end in Germany during the spring of 1899: reports from a small town outside of Bonn revealed that several young women, who had died of unexplained causes, had been seen alive again, but only at night. Van Helsing, welcoming the distraction, left his tour to investigate. Except for one trip to Hong Kong in 1905, he made no further public appearances. The following is Professor Van Helsing's original introduction to his *Field Guide to Monsters*. A gentleman to the end, Van Helsing refrained from speaking ill of Bram Stoker or his novel, but his pain is evident throughout.

ORIGINAL INTRODUCTION TO THE
FIELD GUIDE TO MONSTERS (1898)
By Professor Abraham Van Helsing

T his book that you hold in your hands could very well save your life.

The previous sentence sounds very dramatic, does it not, but this is no work of fiction. I wish it were. It is, however, truly meant to frighten you and I make no apologies for that. I cannot, for Monsters are real, they walk among us right now, and they threaten our very existence. I have made their eradication my life's work.

It was only four hundred years ago that Europe was decimated, almost completely wiped out by the Plague, a disease that began in China and carried by rats across the continents—beasts so tiny and insignificant but with enough poison to kill over a third of the population in Europe. There is now a new disease sweeping across Eastern Europe that has reached even the shores of Great Britain. However, this disease is carried by something far deadlier than rats, and it will take more than another Great Fire to stop it.

This disease is carried by the Living Dead—men and women, once as alive and well as you or I, who have had their very souls ripped from their bodies. Despite having been laid to rest in sacred ground, in a Christian ceremony, these creatures of Hell blaspheme the holy name of God, and rise up to do the Devil's work.

Originated in Transylvania, the disease was reported to have affected the Eastern European dictator Vlad Tepes, the son of Vlad Dracul, a Wallachian. His thirst for human blood was an immortal curse and after he was struck down mortally, dying in a fierce battle, he rose three days later from the dead. Vlad assumed his father's name, and from then on, was known only as Dracula. He had been spreading the disease of blood thirst ever since.

And I pause at this juncture to warn you most strenuously—this is not some fickle work of romance and horror, designed to frighten young women and entertain their swains. This is the unrelenting, unforgiving truth. Dracula has spread his disease of blood thirst across Europe. He has infiltrated entire populations. And, unless we act now, we are all doomed to become enslaved by the same monstrous thirst for human blood. Imagine for one moment, never again being able to walk in the sun. Imagine a life without feeling, without emotion or warmth, without kin, without the light of your immortal soul, or the warmth of the Savior's love within your breast.

While I myself saw Dracula's vile form purged from this world, this victory proved to be a small battle won in an ever-growing war. Much to my horror, Dracula's death did not stop or even hinder the spread of vampires in the world. And, there are other monsters walking the secluded wildernesses of the world, such as werewolves—men, who on the night of the full moon, shed their skins for fur and prey upon mankind for blood and mayhem. While I suspect that there may be some correlation between the werewolf and the vampire to explain their thirst for blood and the importance of the night by which to do these heinous acts, I have only begun to understand these dark mysteries.

But there are far more. There are harpies, witches, demonic lizards, and all manner of things of the air, land, and sea that live to hunt man. It also behooves me to warn all about the "Monster" created by a mad doctor, by the name of Victor Von Frankenstein. I have only made its acquaintance twice and knowing its story, related to me by the late widow of Percy Shelley, I took pity on it. But it is an irrational creature at best and is capable of causing great harm.

Please, I urge you to use this book wisely and do not permit yourself to be deceived by those wishing to terrify you for the sake of entertainment. All our lives depend on it.

We must awake the living before this vile disease awakens all the dead.

Abraham Van Helsing
London, 1898

HOW TO USE THIS BOOK

In "Classifying Monsters," we show you that there are many more creatures walking the Earth than just the vampires listed in Professor Van Helsing's original field guide. So much information has been collated over the last century that was never available to Van Helsing, and the decision to revise his original was a necessity rather than an option. While many have risen to the challenge of taking Van Helsing's place to combat the evils in today's world, more and more creatures and monsters have come out of hiding.

During our ascension to the top of the food chain over the last two hundred years, mankind has expanded and spread out across the face of the entire globe. There are no more uncharted territories or unknown lands for us to find (at least on the Earth's surface). This has made it increasingly difficult for many monsters to remain hidden in their ancient dwellings. Their last refuges from man have been exposed, making these monsters even more dangerous to us. With nowhere left to hide, they are more open about their activities, while the more humanlike creatures find it actually easier to hide in plain sight, preferring it to the hundreds of years of squatting in caves and castle dungeons.

THE LAST REFUGE OF MONSTERS

Monster behavior has also changed in these climates. No longer scared of being revealed, their attacks have become more brazen. And Hollywood has shown us so many monsters that we cannot believe the real thing even when we see it. This was Van Helsing's original fear when Bram Stoker wrote *Dracula* and history has proven the Professor amazingly prescient in this regard.

Behavior is also important when studying vampires since they can appear all too human until it is too late. It is their subtle changes that we have to look out for, not the obvious ones, such as canines protruding down over the bottom lip. Are they eating properly? Do they eat solids? Which of the five food groups are they lacking in? Do you see them during daylight? When was the last time you saw them during a full moon?

EXAMINE YOURSELF CAREFULLY

Please be careful. Negative answers to the above questions may just prove that you (or your child) are a normal teen. Proceed with care; check for allergic reactions to garlic, crucifixes, and churches before trying to force a wooden stake through anyone's heart.

Refer to the sample Monster entries on the opposite page. Each entry shows you where in the world a particular monster has been spotted, what its preferred habitat is, its point of origin, as well as its behavior, strength, powers, and, if any, weaknesses.

CAN YOU OUTWIT THEM?

The "Brain" key located at the top of each page shows your chances of outwitting these beasts. Five brains means that you have no chance in the slightest and run like hell! Half a brain means you might just make it through the night—if you have your wits about you.

Also check out the Size Comparison chart. For creatures that are less than one-quarter the size of a human, we have used this very tome you hold in your hands as an indication of monster height. For creatures larger than this, we have used major world monuments, such the Statue of Liberty. For the rest, we have used a six foot tall man.

AVOID MONSTER HOT SPOTS!

One of the highlights of this guide is the "Observing Monsters" section. This is totally indispensable for those who travel with any frequency. With the widening spread of monsters and creatures, particularly vampires, many airlines and insurance companies are adding clauses in their fine print warning that should you fly into an MHS (Monster Hot Spot), you do so at your own risk. Without realizing it, you or a loved one may be brutally attacked by one of the harpies or get bitten by a vampire, only to learn that the hospital will turn you away for not being covered by your policy. To ensure that this never happens to you, ALWAYS CONSULT OUR GLOBAL CHART BEFORE TRAVEL!! For the wise, a "protection kit" should be the first thing you pack after your toiletries.

While most of the entries in this book are about solitary beings, many do come from larger extended families or are mutations of other creatures. We have done our utmost to bring you the most detailed and updated information possible about all types of monsters, risking life and limb to do so.

Remember, take this guide wherever you go and you'll be able to relax, secure in the knowledge that you are prepared for the worst.

(**Publisher's Note:** While we encourage and support the help and advice given in this book, we do not hold ourselves liable for its misuse or the misunderstandings that can happen through no negligence of either publisher, writer, or reader on use of the book. S#*@ happens. We also hold ourselves exempt from any liability in the eventuality that you may indeed come against a creature or monster that we had no prior information on before going to press).

Info bar

Name

Story

Behavior

Lethality

Weaknesses

Powers

Size comparison

Additional information

Folio

Intelligence
NOTE: Some monsters have dual natures; the brain(s) on the right of the slash indicates the intelligence of the lesser aspect

Annotation

Monster image

Distribution map

CLASSIFYING MONSTERS

Professor Van Helsing's original *Field Guide to Monsters* was a very slim pamphlet devoted mainly to Vampires, with the briefest of mentions to werewolves and man-made creations, such as Doctor Victor Von Frankenstein's experiment, dubbed simply "the Monster." Van Helsing did not think that there needed to be any further classification other than "monster," and he believed only in the existence of creatures that thirsted after human blood, monsters which he called the Living Dead. Frankenstein's walking abomination was the only exception to this, or the only one that the good professor would allow.

As much as the public scoffed at Van Helsing's claims of vampires walking among us, he in turn scoffed at so many of the "myths" of the day that would later be revealed as truth. Thanks to the hard work of so many people, we are finally able to bring you a clearer picture of monster activity across the globe. The number of monsters is increasing every year, and they now exist in almost every region of the world, making the accurate classification of them all the more important.

DRAGONS

Despite Hagrid trying to make them a popular household pet again, dragons do not make good company for children. They have a tendency to burn them to a crisp and then lick up the ashes. Dragons do, however, create close family units and are great fun to watch at play, especially the youngsters, as they practice blowing smoke rings. Some dragons can, in fact, talk and have formed very strong ties to their human companions. Unfortunately, they usually end up sacrificing their lives for their human friends because of something stupid the man does like falling in love with a fair maiden.

WEREWOLVES

The curse of the werewolf is a strange and varied one. For many, the coming of puberty marks the end of their chance for a normal human life. They will find it extremely difficult to be able to stay in one place longer than a month, for with the rising of the full moon, the urge to rip ones clothes off and go running naked down the streets cannot go unheeded. This wouldn't be that much of a problem, except that the desire to then kill and eat anything that moves usually follows.

MUTATED LIFE

The Creature

Triffids

Eight Legged Freaks

Mothra

MUTATED MEN

The Fly

Invisible Man

Hulk

Melting Man

MANUFACTURED

The Monster

Colossus

HAL 9000

RoboCop

SUPERNATURAL

Count Dracula

Hellboy

Slimer

Zombies

FROM THE BEYOND

Creeper

Gizmo

Pinhead

Betelgeuse

MONSTER BEHAVIOR

Most of you will think that establishing a monster's behavior is very obvious and so very easy. When faced with a 300-foot tall fire-breathing lizard looking at turning the entire population of your city into shish kebabs, his motives do certainly seem clear enough. But, it is entirely another matter when you are looking into the eyes of someone you have known all your life, who has loved you, cherished you, worshiped the ground you walked on, and now suddenly wants to eat your brains. Or it simply may be that kid from down the street, the one who always looks at you funny, licking his eyebrows and twitching his ears whenever you walk by. You swear he is looking at you like he can see inside your head, and you get freaked out when you learn that he fits the description of someone who died twelve years ago.

SINGING

Now here you must tread carefully. Many have tried to storm Britney Spears on stage based on the belief that she is a modern-day siren or Pied Piper. No, while she is a monster by normal human standards, she doesn't qualify here. Be more on the look out for singing plants that smack their petals together and stare at you like you are lunchmeat every time you walk past.

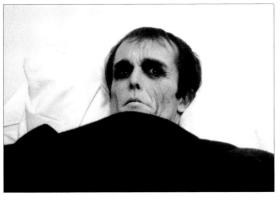

SLEEPING

Or lack thereof. Zombies fall in either or both categories. Their incessant desire to feed on blood and brains causes an even greater loss of cognitive control. Vampires, on the other hand, usually take to sleeping during the daytime and come out only at night, not to be confused with most college students. Other monsters feel a need to rest while their batteries literally need recharging.

INTIMIDATION

Here the behavior of monsters is not dissimilar from your average drunk at a nightclub, who has had three too many drinks and thinks he's the greatest thing since the light-up yo-yo. Both the monster and the drunk have every desire to be seen. Both strike fear in a young girl's heart. But only one of them wants to actually eat it.

FIGHTING

Monsters play dirty. They can't help it; it's in their nature. If they're fighting an unarmed human, they will make the whole thing as torturous as is inhumanly possible. When they're fighting another monster of equal size and strength, they will use any means necessary (like Godzilla here hitting King Kong below the belt) to ensure their victory.

BREEDING

Before some monsters can make love, they first have to make the bride (a slight drawback to being some loon's experiment). The mating rituals can often be long and complicated (and that's not just a case of finding the right body parts to stitch together). Sometimes a monster's idea of a good lay is a thousand eggs in Madison Square Garden. Others merely need to cut off a limb and they instantly regenerate a new mate. While some just opt for biting the girl on the neck or tearing her heart out, others mistakenly go for the more romantic routine of giving a girl a night to remember in the big city. Picking them up, carrying them off breathlessly to the top of the tallest building to dance on the roof by moonlight. Seems like a nice idea until the Air Force shows up.

OBSERVING MONSTERS AND WHERE TO FIND THEM . . .

...presuming, of course, that you are actually looking for them, something we do not recommend. The map below illustrates the hot spots around the world for monster activity.

Very surprising, and worrying indeed, is that these creatures of the damned actually seek out the areas of highest population density (San Francisco, Denver, Washington DC, most of Manhattan, not to mention Hollywood [where it is now widely accepted that more than sixty percent

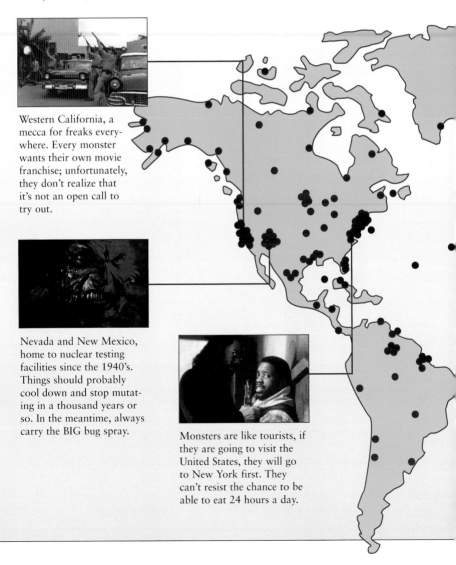

Western California, a mecca for freaks everywhere. Every monster wants their own movie franchise; unfortunately, they don't realize that it's not an open call to try out.

Nevada and New Mexico, home to nuclear testing facilities since the 1940's. Things should probably cool down and stop mutating in a thousand years or so. In the meantime, always carry the BIG bug spray.

Monsters are like tourists, if they are going to visit the United States, they will go to New York first. They can't resist the chance to be able to eat 24 hours a day.

of the inhabitants are monsters]). While, on one hand, this may seem obvious, as they are closer to their primary food source, they also put themselves at a much higher risk of being detected. One can assume that these city-dwelling monsters are not the brightest of the bunch, and that there are more clever and devious monsters hiding in reclusive areas, just waiting for the opportune time to unleash their full fury.

Due to space constraints, we have only indicated the locations of major attacks. For example, while the world has often been plagued with giant insects, lizards, dinosaurs, and the occasional giant ape, it has only really been Asia, in particular Tokyo, that is still leveled on an annual basis by the giant Godzilla.

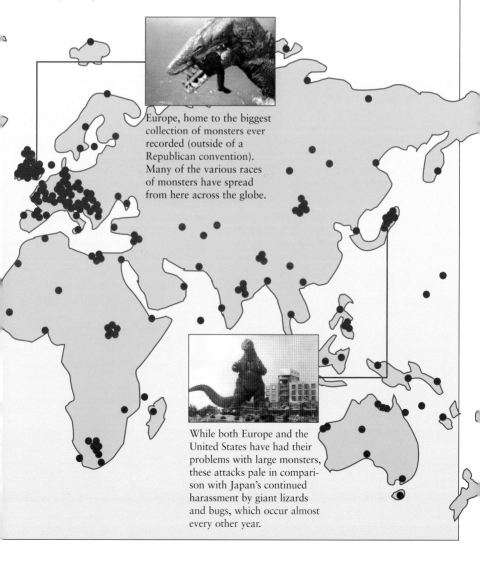

Europe, home to the biggest collection of monsters ever recorded (outside of a Republican convention). Many of the various races of monsters have spread from here across the globe.

While both Europe and the United States have had their problems with large monsters, these attacks pale in comparison with Japan's continued harassment by giant lizards and bugs, which occur almost every other year.

FREQUENTLY ASKED QUESTIONS

Q: If I am bitten by a vampire, is all hope lost?

A: Not always. Several people have made successful recoveries from the vampire's bite. Your chances for survival usually rely on the following:

1. If you have been bitten, but have not yourself tasted the blood of the offending vampire, there is a good chance, with the right care and a transfusion of untainted blood, that you will recover in time. But with some vampires, the virus is transferred via their saliva rather than their blood. If this is the case, try #2.

2. Immediately after being bitten, burn the area of the wound with a red-hot iron and inject or pour raw garlic onto the infected area. This *might* work.

Van Helsing demonstrates the correct way to hold a stake and hammer

3. In some instances, it has been proven that if the offending vampire can be killed before the end of the third day after the first bite, the victim will make a recovery. While being a young female seems to make one a greater target, it also seems that her chances of survival are far greater than for a male victim.

Q: I've noticed a friend of mine has developed hairy palms. Is this the first sign of something I, or rather, he should be worrying about?

A: First check to see what brand of soap your "friend" is using and ask him some blunt questions about his social activities. If he suddenly becomes defensive and starts growling under his breath, turn him into the police before the next full moon. If the police do not take you seriously, then check in with your local office of the Bureau of Paranormal Research and Defense. They should be able to help you out.

Q: Is a stake through the heart the only way to stop a vampire?

A: In his first encounters with vampires, Professor Van Helsing learned that with some, a stake through the heart was really only a temporary death. Remove the stake and the vampire returns to life. Van Helsing then started the tradition of beheading the vampire immediately after staking. Later still, he discovered that vampires react differently to decapitation as well, depending on the amount of time they have spent as a vampire. Older ones would turn into dust, while the younger ones would just stiffen up as rigor mortis set in. But even turning to dust wasn't the end of the vampire. With sufficient blood, dust can be reanimated and the vampire can reform once more.

Q: My partner hasn't blinked for nearly three weeks. He even sleeps with his eyes open wide. What does this mean?

A: It could mean that a spell has been cast and your partner has been turned into a Zombie. It could also mean he was poisoned or ate some bad blowfish (which contains the drug tetrodotoxin, which slowly puts people under a coma). Or, perhaps he simply forgot to take out his contact lenses one night and they're now stuck firmly to his eyeballs.

Q: My doctor, Victor Franks, kept trying to have me sign an organ donor card. I was suspicious at first, but then I found out he was getting all the other patients to do the same. Then, just recently I discovered that six of his patients have died in the last two months. What should I do?

A: Hope you didn't sign one.

Q: Why do crucifixes work?

A: Like most religious symbols, crucifixes, in particular, are the embodiment of everything that is good in the world, something that vampires cannot stand. According to monster historians, the first vampire was actually created by Lilith, the rejected first wife of Adam. Cast out of Eden, she went into the world creating all of the evil creatures of the night.

Q: Which is best for a stake, silver or wood?

A: We polled several vampire slayers, and while not being unanimous, most preferred the silver stake. It makes for a cleaner kill, goes in easily and comes out smoothly, no rough edges, stays sharp, and the blood just rinses off. It also tends to consistently go up in value on the open market.

Q: How can I be sure that the creature is truly dead once I have staked it?

A: You can't. The best you can do is to cut off its head after staking it and to burn the remains. Mix the ashes with garlic, bless them with holy water and then scatter the ashes and skeleton (if there is one) to the four winds. Hey, if it's going to come back anyway, why not make it as difficult as possible?

Q: I keep dreaming that I am being chased in my sleep. When I wake up, I am very sweaty and I have blisters on my feet. What can I do to stop this?

A: Lay off the dairy products before bed. If that doesn't do anything, try taking control of your dreams in a more forceful manner. Many spirits that invade your dreams do so to create fear, which in turn feeds them, so don't give them that chance. As for the blisters, we'd recommend wearing thicker socks and a good pair of running shoes when you go to bed tonight.

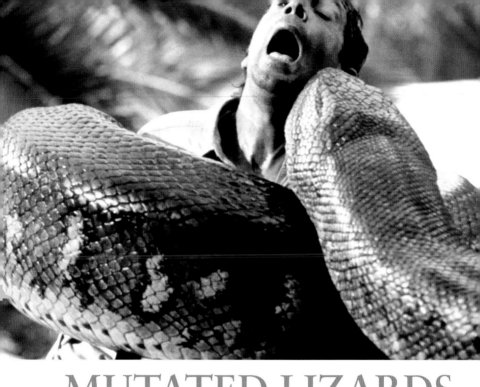

MUTATED LIZARDS,

FISH, AND DINOSAURS

While many of us today may be more aware than ever about the negative effects of pollution and atomic radiation on the environment, there is a similar disparity among the more ignorant members of the population. Chemical spills and radiation experiments still account for a large percentage of mutated monsters. Sometimes the atomic explosions do not cause the mutation itself, but just free something that was long-trapped in the Earth.

Science continues to play its part in the ever-increasing monster population with advances in cloning and organ transplants. Mistakes are continually made and it is usually people like you who have to pay the price. And yet, there was once a time when we wondered innocently about what life was like when dinosaurs ruled the earth. Now, thanks to a large number of scientists, we don't have to wonder, but only run for our lives when we see a hungry T-Rex storming down the boulevard.

The monsters in this section are mainly from the Reptile or Lizard families. They usually prefer to keep to the warmer climates around the world, but there have been a few notable exceptions. One was found living happily in northern England. Proof indeed that monsters must be crazy.

Length: 10-45 feet	Family: *Crocodilian*	Habitat: Swamps; big city sewers
Weight: 900 pounds-1.5 tons	Origin: Tropical and subtropical zones	Intelligence:

ALLIGATOR

Giant alligators are rarely trouble in their natural habitats. Indeed, these nocturnal reptiles are hardly seen even in their native swamps and glades. It is the city alligators that one must avoid. Emotionally damaged and frenetic from having lived an orphaned life in the city's sewer system (flushed down the toilet as infants by uncaring human urbanites), these cold-blooded creatures will go to any lengths to inflict heavy blows on cruel humanity.

BEHAVIOR: Enjoy eating anything from lost pets to portly sewer workers. Not above scavenging for dead animals nor would they snub their noses at cannibalism. A good dose of radiation is always a welcomed snack.

LETHALITY: Incredibly lethal. One of the most powerful bites of any monster, make sure to find a way to secure their jaws first before battling them.

WEAKNESSES: Can be put to sleep by rubbing their bellies. Also harbor a secret fear of luggage stores and leather-bag toting fashionistas.

POWERS: Fang-filled jaws have tremendous crushing power. Massive tails are good for swatting and setting cars on fire.

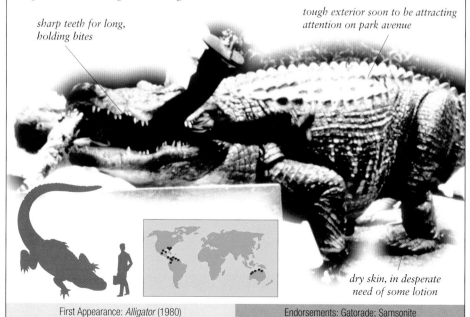

sharp teeth for long, holding bites

tough exterior soon to be attracting attention on park avenue

dry skin, in desperate need of some lotion

First Appearance: *Alligator* (1980)	Endorsements: Gatorade; Samsonite
Relatives: Crocodiles	Appearance: Thick-bellied reptile, ferocious teeth

Length: 40-80 feet	Family: *Boidae*	Habitat: Jungles and rivers
Weight: 300 pounds-1 ton	Origin: South America	Intelligence:

ANACONDA

Normal anacondas are dangerous enough, but when science gone wrong gets done with one, it becomes one of the most terrifying creatures in the South American jungle. In fact, the anaconda is the second most popular reason cited for people's reluctance to travel to South America—beaten out only by the unstable political systems of the region's countries and closely followed by the continent's near total lack of KFC chains.

BEHAVIOR: Likes to swim around and terrorize out-of-towners who ford dangerous and exotic rivers. Greatly enjoys killing loudmouths and actors working for scale.

LETHALITY: Extremely lethal to human beings. No use attacking it head on, best to run quickly around it several times, in the hopes of tangling it into knots.

WEAKNESSES: Cold weather; Gatorland employees.

POWERS: With tremendous jaws, clenches onto its victim, grabs and pulls him underwater. Swims at great speeds, emits a foul-smelling, brownish, poisonous musk, and makes even the toughest of men breakdown and cry like babies.

powerful teeth and jaws, will crush every one of your bones

First Appearance: *Conan the Barbarian* (1982)	Endorsements: Kitchen Crush-O-Matic
Relatives: Eggs a' plenty	Description: Never-ending snake

Height: 20 feet	Family: *Tyrannosauridae*	Habitat: Hollow Mountains
Weight: 10 tons	Origin: Mexico	Intelligence:

BEAST OF HOLLOW MOUNTAIN

The mystery revealed—the Beast of Hollow Mountain is actually a prehistoric Tyrannosaurus Rex anachronistically hiding out in a cave in Hollow Mountain, which is situated in the backcountry of Mexico. This man-eating monster loves to venture out from his cave to feed on local farmers and their cattle, and can be distinguished from other T-Rex dinosaurs by its long drooping tongue that flaps around aimlessly like an eel out of water. Once believed to be a local myth, the Beast is much more than a mere superstition, and if you're ever in Mexico, there's more to be wary of than the country's tap water.

BEHAVIOR: Eats horses and cattle. Uses its absurdly long tongue like an anteater to ward off oily, villainous cattle barons. Also likes ripping the roofs of houses and playing with its inhabitants like dolls.

LETHALITY: If the dinosaur's tongue doesn't get you, the quicksand in the area will.

WEAKNESSES: Not very bright, will fall for any trap.

POWERS: Able to sleep for a million years, suffering only a mild grumpiness and hunger. Nothing a few steers can't fix.

First Appearance: *The Beast of Hollow Mountain* (1956)	Endorsements: Gee-Up Glue
Relatives: All have disowned him	Description: Dinosaur with long tongue

Height: 120 feet	Family: *Rhedosaurus*	Habitat: Oceans and lighthouses
Weight: 50 tons	Origin: Ocean depths	Intelligence:

BEAST FROM 20,000 FATHOMS

From the depths of the ocean, this gargantuan hears and falls in love with the sound of a foghorn, mistaking it for the call of a mate. He surfaces to look for his mate and heads towards New York. But with his love nowhere in sight, Romeo turns into a beastie killing machine, trampling taxicabs and mailboxes, and eating urbanites by the dozen. Worse yet, it has been discovered that he is a carrier of an ancient virulent disease. When military bazookas start gunning for it, the Beast seeks refuge at Coney Island. Severely wounded by this confrontation, he has been spotted a few times cowering underneath roller coasters, perhaps still hoping to unite with his lost love.

water-clogged ears

teeth need brushing

BEHAVIOR: Gullible and lonely. Will accept blind dates from lighthouses.
LETHALITY: Extremely dangerous to humans. Eats them by the dozen and carries a disease killing the rest. Demolishes busloads of people with its massive tail and feet.
WEAKNESSES: Can't tell the difference between machine noises and potential mates. Easily handled by the military.
POWERS: Massively strong. Can breathe underwater for extended periods. Fish breath can empty a stadium faster than the Captain and Tennille.

| Height: 8 feet | Family: *Brachyura* | Habitat: Castles |
| Weight: 1-2 tons | Origin: Under the sea | Intelligence: |

CRAB MONSTERS

Mutants with a crippling weakness for human brains, these stalk-eyed decapods actually grow more intelligent as they consume mammalian gray matter. So smart, in fact, that they have formed a strategy—cutting down on the chase time, they will actually munch away at the ground below your feet. Huge and vicious, these crab monsters are quite aggressive eaters; don't under-estimate them. It has been documented that they can finish off several square miles of rock in a few days.

can smell a human brain from miles away

mandibles that specialize in cutting the tops of heads off

BEHAVIOR: Inhabits islands occupied by explorers, researchers, and castaways. Will attack people instantly to get at those yummy brains.

LETHALITY: Quite lethal. Ability to communicate telepathically grows with every human brain consumed. Will slaughter anyone from Mother Teresa to Santa Claus on sight.

WEAKNESSES: Boiling water and extremely large pliers. Will run at the sight of a lobster bib.

POWERS: Armored bodies. Fantastically sharp claws with tremendous crushing power. Able to read minds.

| First Appearance: *Attack of the Crab Monsters* (1957) | Endorsements: Red Lobster |
| Relatives: The buffet at Beefsteak Charlie's | Description: Jumbo seafood |

| Height: 7 feet | Family: *Reptilicus Sapien* | Habitat: Amazon River |
| Weight: 290 pounds | Origin: South America | Intelligence: |

CREATURE FROM THE BLACK LAGOON

The Creature from the Black Lagoon, otherwise known as "Gillman," is discovered by an expedition searching for missing links to mankind's past. A monstrous creature from the deep, Gillman has to be one of the ugliest among all the monsters. Bright green all over, and covered with large gills (hence, Gillman), he seems to think that wearing red lipstick will help him score some points with the ladies.

*sensitive eyes
(seek sensitive girl)*

BEHAVIOR: Normally swims around and catches fish. Enjoys the sun. Likes to study boats from afar. Seeks female for cozy twosome. Would prefer a willing one, but not a deal breaker.

sixteen-pack abs

LETHALITY: Dangerous to human males or unattractive females when they get in the way of its courting of beauty queens.

WEAKNESSES: Very slow out of the water. Not very good at avoiding nets. Girls in bathing suits.

POWERS: Can remain submerged underwater indefinitely. Powerful body covered with tough scales. Has terrible claws and a face that would frighten Frankenstein's monster.

| First Appearance: *Creature from the Black Lagoon* (1954) | Endorsements: Snorkel Hut |
| Relatives: Most of the residents of Innsmouth | Description: Enlarged gills, red lips |

Height: Hand-sized	Family: *Serrasalminae*	Habitat: The Amazon
Weight: A few ounces	Origin: South America	Intelligence:

PIRANHAS

Millions of flesh-eating mutant piranhas are loose in the nation's reservoirs and rivers. Created by a military project dubbed "Operation Razorteeth," these miniature killers enjoy terrorizing summer camps, and especially look to nibble on young girls in bikinis. Now they have infiltrated sewer systems and are waiting with the alligators to bite off the limbs of sanitation workers. Small enough, these buggers have even been known to leap out of toilets and faucets.

can smell human flesh from underwater

tiny sharp teeth, plus strong-locking jaws

BEHAVIOR:
Mindlessly looking everywhere for their next meal. One form of mutated Piranha could actually fly, multiplying their food base. Basically, these are just very hungry little scamps.

LETHALITY:
As dangerous as blind pit bulls in a locked room filled with people covered in bacon grease. Perfectly willing to eat anyone they can sink their teeth into down to the bone and beyond.

WEAKNESSES: Can be poisoned, that's about it (don't even make good soup). Scared only by Florida tourist storeowners who lacquer and mount them on their walls.

POWERS: Razor-sharp teeth, instinctively attack in overwhelming schools. Some varieties can fly, while others have legs and opposable thumbs.

First Appearance: *Piranha* (1978)	Endorsements: In negotiations with Fear Factor
Relatives: By the riverfull	Description: Little fish with protruding teeth

| Length: 12-55 feet | Family: *Crocodilian* | Habitat: Swamps, marshes, and moats |
| Weight: 1-2.5 tons | Origin: Tropical Zone | Intelligence: |

CROCODILE

Giant crocodiles can be found around all manner of questionable modern facilities. If there is a leaking vat of suspicious chemicals, an illegally dumped canister of bad toxin, or any other corporate biological mistake nearby, you can bet dollars to doughnuts that a crocodile will get its pointed snout in there somehow and be barn-sized by lunchtime.

big, big, thick jaw muscles for biting dinner in two

note the more pointed snout over his cousin, the alligator

rinsing his mouth out after breakfast

BEHAVIOR: Lots of snarling and roaring. Love to chase pirate ships in hopes of snapping up body parts.

LETHALITY: Plenty dangerous. Irrational, tiny reptilian brain keeps these leathery jokers snapping at everything in sight.

WEAKNESSES: Dumb as stumps. Tie their jaws shut, and they don't have a chance.

POWERS: Powerful jaws, thick skin. Can trick many to sympathy with their ability to cry on cue.

| First Appearance: *Peter Pan* (1953) | Endorsements: Gatorland; Peter Pan Peanut Butter |
| Relatives: Fantasia dance troupe | Description: Greenish gray reptile |

Height: 10-100 feet	Family: *Iguanodon*
Weight: 1,000 pounds-5 tons	Origin: China

DRAGONS

Dragons have been with mankind since the beginning. The first recorded mention of them comes from the Bible—not only as creatures in their own right, but also as one of the alternate names for Satan. Fabulous monsters variously represented, but most often depicted as huge, winged reptiles with crested heads, terrible claws, and the ability to breath fire. Dragons are such legendary creatures, staples in multiple cultural myths, that their lethality is almost completely forgotten by the general population.

BEHAVIOR: Western dragons run amok, peeling open suits of armor or SUVs for the delicate morsels inside, or burning crops and buildings, looking for treasure. Eastern dragons tend more to harmless pursuits, studying with monks, playing with kites, conversing with clouds, and creatures that live above the cloud line.

LETHALITY: All dragons are massively powerful, and possess great claws, which can do tremendous damage.

WEAKNESSES: Can be lured out of the deepest cave by the scent of a chained virgin. Defenseless against missiles or tank shells. Indeed, even a well-placed shot from an elephant rifle should be able to stop any dragon in its tracks.

POWERS: Flight, flame-thrower breath, and massive strength. Ability to assess worth of precious metals and gems with the naked eye.

red, hot fire-breath

First Appearance: *Siegfried* (1924)

Relatives: Elliot, from Pete's Dragon

Habitat: Caves

Intelligence:

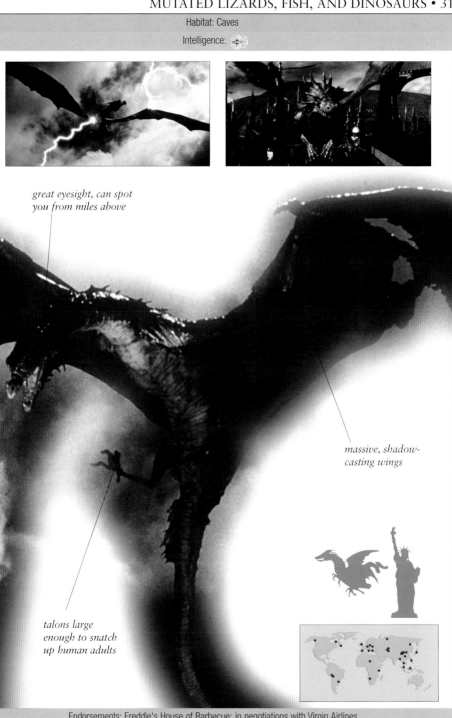

great eyesight, can spot you from miles above

massive, shadow-casting wings

talons large enough to snatch up human adults

Endorsements: Freddie's House of Barbecue; in negotiations with Virgin Airlines

Description: Scaly; various colors

| Height: 164-328 feet | Family: Giant Reptilian |
| Weight: 22,000-66,000 tons | Origin: Japan |

GODZILLA

The monster Gojira tears through Japan for no logical reason—not because of hunger, revenge, anger, conquest, or hatred. Can nothing explain this massive wave of destruction? Oh yes, it is man and his playing God with the creation of the atomic bomb. Did the bomb awaken this lumbering monster from an ancient slumber or is this giant radioactive lizard purely a creation of this nuclear weapons fallout? Whatever it is, Gojira (or Godzilla as it is pronounced in the West) is here to stay. Many times, he has risen to attack the city of Tokyo and, with the same mentality of those who choose to live in California, the people of Japan rebuild and carry on as though nothing has happened. Even the dreaded oxygen destroyer fails to stop the fire-breathing modern-day dragon, leading many to think of Godzilla as an elemental force, like a hurricane or earthquake.

radioactive armor-plating

First Appearance: *Gojira (1954)*

Relatives: Son, Minilla (adopted)

Habitat: Islands and peninsulas

Intelligence:

BEHAVIOR: Favorite activities include destroying miniature Japanese cities, duking it out with other colossal creatures and hibernating for centuries on end.

LETHALITY: Very dangerous to humans and their dwellings. Incredibly heavy, as well as radioactive. Capable of expelling streams of forceful radioactive breath that melt everything in its path.

WEAKNESSES: A brain the size of a walnut. Easily distracted by electricity, tanks, and other petty obstacles.

POWERS: Atomic ray breath, super regenerative abilities, nuclear pulse, shrugs off machine gun and tank fire, as well as rockets and staggering amounts of electricity.

spikes make sleeping on his back very painful

Endorsements: In negotiations with North Korea and Thailand

Description: Green sea monster with spikes on back

| Height: 100 feet | Family: *Gorgosaurus* | Habitat: Deep blue sea |
| Weight: 10 tons | Origin: Waters off Ireland | Intelligence: |

GORGO

Nara Island is the site of a terrible storm and the eruption of an underwater volcano. The combined disasters awaken a gorgosaurus and send it lumbering onto land where it destroys everything in sight. Some enterprising sailors capture the baby gorgon and exhibit it in a London circus. A good idea until Gorgo's considerably more lethal mama comes looking for it.

BEHAVIOR: Walks around stiffly as if its arms don't move properly. Tramples on anything in its path. Screams like a banshee at feeding time.
LETHALITY: Not purposely lethal to humans, but tends to kill many when it steps on buildings and refuses to yield the right-of-way to oncoming cars.
WEAKNESSES: Eyes easily blinded by shining light.
POWERS: Great jaws and claws, with massive size and strength should make Gorgo a world-class monster, but it only seems to enjoy stepping on things.

thick rubber neck of a football quarterback

| First Appearance: *Gorgo* (1961) | Endorsements: Playschool Baby Leashes |
| Relatives: Mama Gorgo | Description: Toddler-sized sea monster |

| Height: Varies | Family: Dinosaur | Habitat: Desert |
| Weight: Varies | Origin: Mexico | Intelligence: |

GWANGI & FRIENDS

In Mexico, the discovery of an Eohippus, a prehistoric ancestor to the modern horse, leads to an even greater discovery of a lost world. In a valley cut off from the world for the last sixty-five million years, prehistoric creatures of all types live in bliss unaware that outside the boundaries of their high-walled domain the mammals have taken over. Circus owners, however, continually venture into this preserved ancient world to capture the highly sought-after creatures dwelling there. The Tyrannosaurs Rex, for instance, would be the catch of the century.

BEHAVIOR: Perfectly willing to act like enraged dinosaurs at the least provocation. Will eat or sleep at the drop of a pith helmet.
LETHALITY: Incredibly dangerous to human, whose mere existence seems to set these prehistoric monsters off.
WEAKNESSES: Computer illiterate. Couldn't download an escape route out of their valley from Mapquest to save their souls.
POWERS: Fangs, claws, great strength, the usual

powerful teeth can bite into the leathery backs of elephants

cute little baby hands

| First Appearance: *The Valley of Gwangi* (1969) | Endorsements: GatorLand |
| Relatives: The Wide World of Reptiles | Description: Varies |

Height: 15 feet	Family: Ye Olde Horrors	Habitat: Found around the base of trees
Weight: 3 tons	Origin: Ancient Greece	Intelligence:

HYDRA

The Hydra is a monstrous, nine-headed serpent woman who has the power to turn men into stone. The stench from her breath is also potent enough to kill the mightiest of warriors, and if this isn't bad enough, she can produce whole legions of skeleton soldiers from her teeth! Of her nine heads, one can never be harmed, which makes killing her almost impossible, and any heads that are successfully cut off usually grow back within a few days.

BEHAVIOR: Easily disturbed. Craves male attention.
LETHALITY: This perpetually angry monster seems to have it in for everyone and everything that comes close enough to bite. Nasty, moody, and violent, this thing is one to be avoided at all costs.
WEAKNESSES: Apparently quite susceptible to direct sword thrusts to the chest.
POWERS: Multiple heads with strong beaks, tremendous crushing power in its tail, and a terrible, terrible temper.

cut off a head and another shall take its place

searing hot acid for saliva

First Appearance: *Jason and the Argonauts* (1963)	Endorsements: In negotiations with Hydrox Cookies
Relatives: Freshwater polyps constituting the Hydra genus	Description: Seven-headed snakewoman

Length: 35 feet	Family: *Carcharodon carcharlas*	Habitat: Coastlines of resort towns
Weight: 1.5 tons	Origin: Deep blue sea	Intelligence: 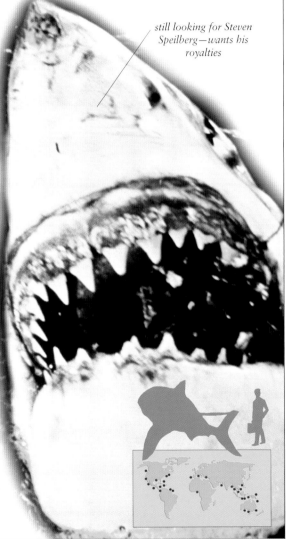

JAWS

The killing spree of this white shark, which some have dubbed Jaws, first started in Amity, a small resort island in New England. He targets young, promiscuous swimmers, especially those who like to skinny-dip. Once Jaws has bitten into his victim, he'll throw that person about, back and forth, breaking off limbs one by one, and he won't stop until the blue water is completely changed to blood red. This shark is so scary that he even has his own scary theme song. If you ever hear it while you are swimming in the ocean, it's because Jaws already has plans to make you into dinner.

still looking for Steven Speilberg—wants his royalties

BEHAVIOR: Mindlessly swims about tearing limbs from people, chomping out holes in boats, swallowing license plates and anything else that it can find.
LETHALITY: Quite dangerous to human beings and seaside economies. Loves to tear off an arm from one person, then just let it sink to the bottom of the ocean while it swallows someone else's shoulder. Irrationality as a hunter makes its next move impossible to predict.
WEAKNESSES: Electricity, boiling water, large explosions, and spear guns.
POWERS: Great swimmer, able to stay submerged with three empty barrels attached, powerful jaws, hypnotic doll-like eyes.

First Appearance: *Jaws* (1975)	Endorsements: Mack's Fine Cutlery; Shoji's Shark-Fin Soup
Relatives: Jaws II; Jaws 3-D; Deep Blue Sea; Hook-jaw	Description: White with sharp teeth

| Length: 30 feet | Family: *Plesiosaur* | Habitat: Lochs (of course) |
| Weight: 5 tons | Origin: Scotland | Intelligence: |

THE LOCH NESS MONSTER

The Loch Ness Monster, fondly referred to as "Nessie," is an elusive sea monster found in the Lochs of Scotland. Incredibly camera shy, Nessie hates the paparazzi, and it has revealed itself to only a small number of humans, among them being American zoologist Jonathan Dempsey. Dempsey, who initially traveled to Scotland to disprove Nessie's existence, was shocked to discover that not only is Nessie real, but it is also magical. But keep in mind, the Loch Ness is no creature to fool around with. Though surprisingly gentle for its size, it does like to turn over boats with its great hump, and sneak up on unsuspecting swimmers with its incredibly long tail.

BEHAVIOR: Swims around a lot, mostly out-of-sight. This J.D. Salinger of the monster set loves to tease photographers with its rare and brief appearances.
LETHALITY: To date this docile dino has posed no reported threat to humanity. Kelp and trout are about the only things in danger when Nessie swims by.
WEAKNESSES: Incredibly shy, doesn't understand the first thing about self-promotion.
POWERS: Great swimmer, can apparently hold its breath for decades on end.

little horns on head for decoration

Nessie introduces herself to local children.

| First Appearance: *Loch Ness* (1996) | Endorsements: Scottish Airways |
| Relatives: The Loch Ness Quintuplets | Description: Smiling sea monster with large eyes |

Length: 80 feet	Family: *O.gladiator*	Habitat: Shadowy coves
Weight: 6 tons	Origin: The frigid North Atlantic	Intelligence:

ORCA

Orca is the killer whale that takes vengeance to a whole new level. After losing his mate and unborn baby to Captain Nolan's harpoon, Orca has never really been the same. Blinded by hate and rage, the Orca's thirst for revenge has become dangerously insatiable. He went after Nolan, destroying his ships and killing his crewmen, but out for more blood, the Orca has taken to attacking aquariums, and holding their audiences hostage for lucrative ransoms.

BEHAVIOR: Irrational and murderous with ferocious appetites. Strikes fear in the hearts of many.
LETHALITY: Quite deadly to humans, takes vengeance very seriously.
WEAKNESSES: Harpoons, saunas, girls holding out little fishes high above the water.
POWERS: Fast swimmer, able to hold breath for extended periods. Powerful jaws filled with dachshund-sized teeth.

thick-skinned

hires himself out for fraudulent insurance claims

First Appearance: *Orca (1977)*	Endorsements: SeaWorld
Relatives: Willie	Description: Slippery-skinned whale

Height: 85 feet	Family: God	Habitat: Pyramids; Art Deco buildings
Weight: 2 tons	Origin: Mexico	Intelligence:

Q

Quetzalcoatl is the feathered serpent god that was once worshipped by the Aztec and the Toltec—which isn't saying much since both cultures have been extinct for thousands of years. Without his regular fan base, Quetzalcoatl had nothing else to do but sleep. It would have probably been in hibernation for the rest of eternity, if it wasn't for one sadistic fool who decided to summon forth the flesh-eating bird deity to wreak havoc in the Big Apple (it's always one person that ruins it for everyone else). Now Quetzalcoatl is roosting in the rookery of midtown Manhattan's famed Chrysler Building, hatching devilish plans for world domination.

BEHAVIOR: Cruising uptown neighborhoods for warm-blooded flesh to feast on. Anything from bathing beauties and unattended doggies to construction workers and gangsters: if it has a Type O pulse, it's ready for breakfast. Particular favorite is young girls in rooftop swimming pools.

LETHALITY: Extremely dangerous to all humans who venture out on rooftops. Bad news for the cable television repair industry.

WEAKNESSES: Bullets, conquistadors.

POWERS: Can fly with the grace of a gull, move as quietly as a hummingbird, and rip apart an entire football team in a matter of minutes with its razor teeth and claws.

messy eater

First Appearance: *Q: The Winged Serpent* (1982)	Endorsements: Q-Tips
Relatives: One Dozen Really Extra Large Eggs	Description: Orange-colored, flying predator

Length: 5 feet 8 inches	Family: *Reptilicus Sapien*	Habitat: Small rural towns
Weight: 185 pounds	Origin: England	Intelligence:

REPTILE

Cursed by the Snake People of Borneo, Anna Franklyn is turned into the Reptile—a monster that can change from a young beautiful woman to a man-eating snake hybrid in seconds. Found near Cornwall, England, the Reptile sheds her scaly skin every winter and slithers into town to feed on the locals. A frequent patron of pubs, she likes to prey upon helpless men who have had too much to drink. Her tongue is full of venom, so better to resist her charms completely.

reptile eyes can see into ultraviolet range

BEHAVIOR: Plays the sitar. Curls up in front of fires, ends up getting frustrated trying to climb into someone's warm shoes. Keeps a lot of small pets that don't tend to live too long.

LETHALITY: Very lethal bite. Poison must be cut out immediately after bite for hope of recovery. Can change from beautiful young woman to snake woman very fast.

WEAKNESSES: Venom only good for one bite at a time; shoots its load too quickly. Susceptible to cold temperatures.

POWERS: Poisonous bite, scales, and super strength makes this creature very formidable.

fangs can puncture through anything

First Appearance: *Reptile* (1966)	Endorsements: Various Snake oil brands
Relatives: Cousin appeared in Harry Potter	Description: Woman with reptile face

| Height: 164 feet | Family: Giant Reptilian |
| Weight: 16,500 tons | Origin: Japan |

RODAN

Awakened by miners, this slumbering nightmare was quick to take to the skies over Japan so that it could then kill everyone in sight. It is one of the meanest of monsters—one who, unlike Godzilla, never found itself basking in a happy thought even once (other than the undiluted joy of killing hundreds of people).

Rodan wreaks havoc and destruction

BEHAVIOR: Flies around looking for things to destroy and people to kill. When it finds them, it destroys them, and then goes off looking for more.

LETHALITY: Extremely dangerous to humans. Willing to tear them apart, drop them from great heights, eat them, and caw incessantly until it makes their ears bleed.

WEAKNESSES: Not bright, could easily be tricked into flying into a window and knocking itself out. If only there were windows that big.

POWERS: Flies at Mach 1.5, nearly indestructible wing can create devastating windstorms. Can drop guano bombs the size of football fields.

First Appearance: *Rodan* (1956)

Relatives: Dragons

Habitat: Mountaintops

Intelligence: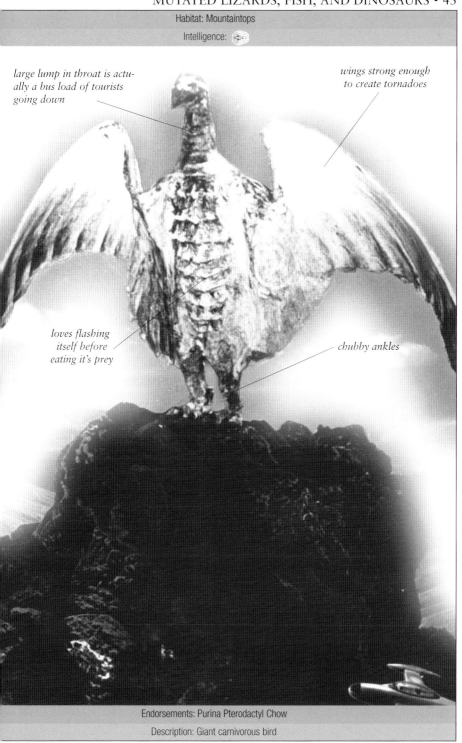

large lump in throat is actually a bus load of tourists going down

wings strong enough to create tornadoes

loves flashing itself before eating it's prey

chubby ankles

Endorsements: Purina Pterodactyl Chow

Description: Giant carnivorous bird

Length: 300 feet	Family: *Decapod*	Habitat: Bottom of the deep blue sea
Weight: 100 tons	Origin: Deep blue sea	Intelligence:

SQUID

Giant squids, long believed to be a myth, are now known to populate the bottom of all the world's oceans. From time to time, when novelists or screenwriters have needed an especially fearsome aquatic monster, these oddly designed cephalopods have been called upon to attack submarines, destroy bridges, and even come out of the sea to run amok in pre-homosexual San Francisco.

BEHAVIOR: Grabs onto anything in the water with monstrously strong tentacles. Prefers large vessels and inanimate structures to actual edible items, except when appearing on television where its appetite for human flesh shows itself more rapidly.

LETHALITY: Tremendously powerful limbs can crush almost anything they wrap around, especially when the giant squid has been exposed to radiation. Enormous beak, designed by nature to rip its prey apart, also usually not brought into use unless TV cameras are nearby.

WEAKNESSES: Harpoons, hot oil, nuclear radiation (causes massive growth but reduces number of tentacles).

POWERS: Great swimmer, can stay submerged at fantastic depths for extended periods, can do reasonable impression of a giant octopus for audiences that are not that bright.

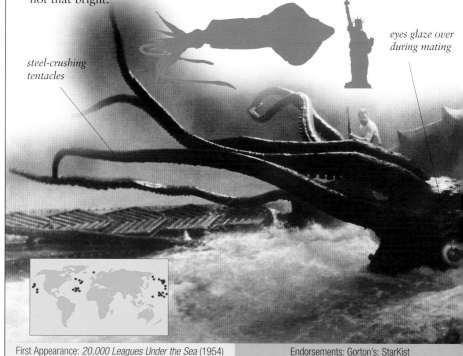

steel-crushing tentacles

eyes glaze over during mating

First Appearance: *20,000 Leagues Under the Sea* (1954)	Endorsements: Gorton's; StarKist
Relatives: Nets full of cuttlefish	Description: Tentacles and roaming eyeballs

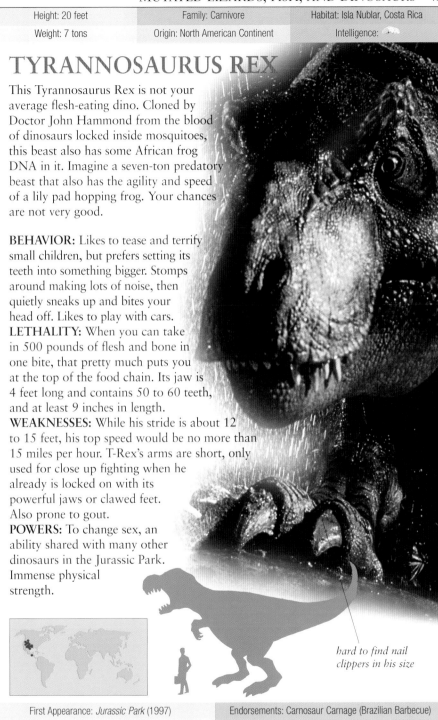

| Height: 20 feet | Family: Carnivore | Habitat: Isla Nublar, Costa Rica |
| Weight: 7 tons | Origin: North American Continent | Intelligence: |

TYRANNOSAURUS REX

This Tyrannosaurus Rex is not your average flesh-eating dino. Cloned by Doctor John Hammond from the blood of dinosaurs locked inside mosquitoes, this beast also has some African frog DNA in it. Imagine a seven-ton predatory beast that also has the agility and speed of a lily pad hopping frog. Your chances are not very good.

BEHAVIOR: Likes to tease and terrify small children, but prefers setting its teeth into something bigger. Stomps around making lots of noise, then quietly sneaks up and bites your head off. Likes to play with cars.

LETHALITY: When you can take in 500 pounds of flesh and bone in one bite, that pretty much puts you at the top of the food chain. Its jaw is 4 feet long and contains 50 to 60 teeth, and at least 9 inches in length.

WEAKNESSES: While his stride is about 12 to 15 feet, his top speed would be no more than 15 miles per hour. T-Rex's arms are short, only used for close up fighting when he already is locked on with its powerful jaws or clawed feet. Also prone to gout.

POWERS: To change sex, an ability shared with many other dinosaurs in the Jurassic Park. Immense physical strength.

hard to find nail clippers in his size

| First Appearance: *Jurassic Park* (1997) | Endorsements: Carnosaur Carnage (Brazilian Barbecue) |
| Relatives: T-Rex from The Lost World; Jurassic Park 3 | Description: Purple and gray |

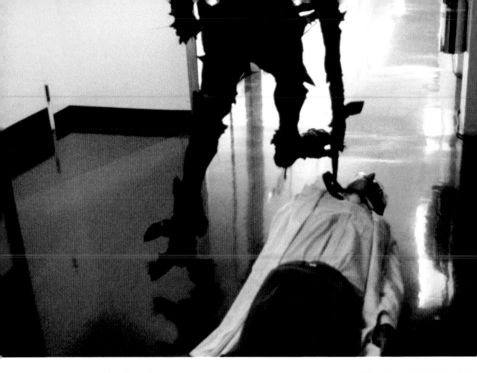

MUTATED MEN, WOMEN,

ANIMALS, AND INSECTS

Either blinded by personal ambition or merely the belief that their work is worth innocent lives, certain scientists never seem to see the catastrophic repercussions to their experiments. And they fail to learn from their mistakes.

Whatever it is, men of science have always been willing to risk the effects of an experiment on another person, animal, or insect without taking into account the possibilities of failure, and what effect that their creation may have on the rest of the world. There are now several documented cases, most of which you will find in this volume, of scientists who have even gone as far as to experiment on themselves. These men, when faced with obstacles such as the loss of funding, prove their commitment and ideals by risking their very lives to complete their work. Unfortunately, scientists do not work well under this kind of pressure. So many are entranced by their genius that they overlook something so minor, like the fact that a fly has flown into their machine, thereby changing the entire experiment with disastrous results.

Of course, we cannot blame these human beings for everything. In some instances, we may find that a greater evil was at work within the human heart, a darkness that was hiding within, just waiting for the right time to assume control.

| Height: 70 feet | Family: Human | Habitat: Modern Cities |
| Weight: Putting on the pounds | Origin: California | Intelligence: |

AMAZING COLOSSAL MAN

After being exposed to a large vat of radiation, good ol' G.I. Glenn Manning (a.k.a. Amazing Colossal Man) finds himself alive when he should have been dead. In fact, he keeps on growing, except for his hair, which falls out. But his body and mind can't keep pace with the growth. His blood just isn't carrying enough oxygen to his gray matter. When his growth stops, at around 70 feet, his mind snaps and he goes completely insane. Escaping the hospital and authorities, he has been spotted in Las Vegas wreaking havoc on casinos and cocktail waitresses, after being turned away at the Sands Casino (couldn't get tickets to see Sinatra).

BEHAVIOR: Starts acting erratically as he grows larger, can't remember where he left his car keys. Wears oversized diapers. Sore loser at Blackjack.
LETHALITY: Doesn't always pay attention to what he's knocking over.

man enough to wear oversized diapers

the original barbie

WEAKNESSES: Still thinks that he has a chance with a woman less than one-tenth his size.
POWERS: Does a foul temper count?

| First Appearance: *The Amazing Colossal Man* (1957) | Endorsements: Jolly Green Giant |
| Relatives: Colossus of New York | Description: BIG |

Height: 7 feet 6 inches	Family: Canine	Habitat: The Moors
Weight: 300 pounds	Origin: Devonshire, England	Intelligence:

HOUND OF THE BASKERVILLES

If you're ever walking in the Moors, and you hear the ghostly howling of a hound from the distance, don't bother running. The Hound can track you from miles away—the stink of sweat and fear being quite pungent to its bloodhound snout. Better to appease it with links of sausages or a giant squeaking ball. Tied, starved, and mistreated by its master, the Hound, which has haunted the Baskerville family for generations, is one beast to be avoided at all costs. If you see the Hound, throw a stick as far as you can, and then run the other way!

BEHAVIOR: Baying at the moon. Chewing up shoes (while they're still on people's feet).
LETHALITY: Slobber a man to death in two minutes.
WEAKNESSES: Has to keep stopping to bark at full moons and, of course, there's the occasional tree.
POWERS: Very strong and powerful, can bring a man down with ease.

Sherlock Holmes and crew

lucky tooth

First Appearance: *Hound of the Baskervilles* (1939)	Endorsements: Well's "Food of the Dogs"
Relatives: Clifford the Big Red Dog	Description: Black; protruding fangs of death

| Length: 30 feet | Family: Insect | Habitat: Catacombs |
| Weight: 4 tons | Origin: New Mexico | Intelligence: |

GIANT ANT

Giant ants are running loose in the city! After several people go missing, after having the roofs torn from their homes, police officer Ben Peterson teams up with FBI agent Bob Graham to find out what's behind the strange disappearances. Taking a cast of a footprint found in one of the crime scenes, they are dumbfounded to find out that the perpetrator is a giant ant. The only known cause of this mutant variety is an atomic test that took place nine years ago. Though most of the original giant ants, along with their nest, have been destroyed, two queens and a couple of drones were able to escape and have thus procreated like hell!

powerful mandibles

BEHAVIOR: Wherever there is sugar, you'll find THEM.
LETHALITY: Huge pincers, fantastic strength and speed. Don't let them see you in wide, open spaces.
WEAKNESSES: United States Army.
POWERS: They're huge, what more do you want?

hairy legs for picking up sugar

| First Appearance: *Them!* (1954) | Endorsements: Atomic Energy Commission |
| Relatives: Eggs everywhere | Description: Giant Black Ant |

Height: 1/4 inch	Family: Ant	Habitat: Jungle
Weight: Next to nothing	Origin: South America	Intelligence:

KILLER ANTS

Hundreds of millions of red army ants have infested the South American continent. Who knows where they came from, or how they managed to build up an army so quickly? One thing is for sure, they're determined to rule the world. No longer satisfied with digging little holes underground, and being labeled as "those hard little workers," these ants are clearly tired of being stepped on by the rest of creation. Christopher Leiningen, a cocoa plantation owner, knows firsthand the terrible wrath of these revolutionary ants—he almost lost his life to these biting monsters as they covered him from head to toe. Scary, determined little creatures, these red ants can march across any terrain, as rough as the Amazon jungle, and like soldiers, they form lines that are more than twenty miles long and two miles wide. They devour everything along the way, and cross rivers by using themselves as bridges.

BEHAVIOR: Relentless with soldier mentality, will trek across any terrain. Eat anything as they go. Won't stop their destruction to rest or appreciate the scenery. They like more than just sugar water, they'll bite into your flesh with their teeny tiny teeth.

LETHALITY: When faced with millions and millions of them—pretty lethal! Twenty miles long and two miles wide, they're going to get you.

WEAKNESSES: Dynamite, water, fire, Hollywood budgets, Hollywood-manufactured love.

POWERS: Teeth, billions of them.

if you look carefully you can see them clicking their little jaws with eager anticipation

First Appearance: *The Naked Jungle* (1954)	Endorsements: Farmer Amos Ant Farms
Relatives: In every kitchen	Description: Red insects

Height: 6 feet 6 inches	Family: Gorilla	Habitat: Las Vegas shows
Weight: 408 pounds	Origin: Africa	Intelligence:

APE

Wise mutant ape (called Ape, of course) is the adoptive guardian of George, King of the Jungle (your modern-day Tarzan). Ape is also apparently British. And he did his best to raise George right and to teach him manners and enough English to get by on should company drop in. But George, not being the brightest, didn't make it easy. All grown up, George falls in love with American noblewoman, Ursula Stanhope, whom he saves from man-eating lions. They leave the jungle together, and after a dramatic situation with Ursula's villainous ex, Ape ends up joining them as well. Currently, Ape is said to be the toast of Las Vegas.

thick fur protects his body, but prefers blue satin suits

BEHAVIOR: Constantly reading and trying to get George to remember things he's told him.

LETHALITY: Don't stand up wind of him.

WEAKNESSES: Bananas and show tunes.

POWERS: Super physical strength, and a great singing voice.

las vegas life style is taking its toll

First Appearance: *George of the Jungle* (1997)	Endorsements: The Sands, Las Vegas
Relatives: Amy, Cheetah	Description: Dominant male ape

| Height: 5 feet 6 inches | Family: Orangutan | Habitat: Congress; malls |
| Weight: 200 pounds | Origin: Zoo | Intelligence: |

DOCTOR ZAIUS

Doctor Zaius, leader of the apes, is determined to rule the planet once more. A civilized, lingual and ruthless leader, he will do anything to keep humans down (perhaps because he can't stand the thought of being ruled by a species that would blow themselves up). He is known to shoot any man or woman on sight, and quite enjoys performing experiments and probes on his prisoners.

BEHAVIOR: Loves ordering lobotomies on anything that can scratch its own ass. Hides behind his doctrine.
LETHALITY: Gorillas are very violent hawks in this society, and the chimpanzees are all bleeding heart liberals. But it is the Orangutans that you have to watch out for, always preferring to use others to do their dirty work.
WEAKNESSES: Bananas, crazy hatred of humans.
POWERS: Rides horses and can still swing from the trees.

blond hairy chest

Dr. Zaius' mug shot

| First Appearance: *Planet of the Apes* (1968) | Endorsements: Tango |
| Relatives: Treesfull | Description: Elderly primate with blond hair and beard |

Height: 6 feet 8 inches	Family: Mythical man-beast	Habitat: Catacombs and caves
Weight: 300 pounds	Origin: Catacombs under Manhattan	Intelligence:

BEAST

Vincent is a man-beast who lives underground in a secret community of outcasts beneath New York City. He must hide from the outside world because of his grotesque appearance and, though it is rumored that he is a genuinely nice guy, with a heart of gold (not to mention a big softie when it comes to his one true love Catherine), his beastly face is enough to send anyone reeling. Unlike the fairytale, the Beast here does not change into a handsome prince after the fair maiden falls in love with him. Instead, he remains a monster on the outside, but now he is more willing to show people his inner beauty.

girls can't resist rock-star hair

BEHAVIOR: Moody, sulks a lot. Hides in the shadows and makes it very difficult to find him when you want him. Refuses to have a cell phone.

LETHALITY: Only hurts those who wish to harm him or his friends.

WEAKNESSES: Blondes.

POWERS: Strength and cunning intellect.

Vincent and Catherine

| Height: 9 feet | Family: Under debate | Habitat: Forests, mountains, suburbia |
| Weight: 400 pounds | Origin: Under debate | Intelligence: |

BIG FOOT

Big Foot is but one name for a race of creatures that have been sighted around the world for thousands of years, known also as Yeti, Sasquatch, Linebacker, and so on. These elusive beasts have been labeled as everything from the missing links and surviving Neanderthals to government experiments and alien invaders.

BEHAVIOR: The Big Foots of the world seem only to wish to be left alone. They avoid all contact with humanity whenever possible. They leave no footprints or droppings for anyone to find, and run (or at least quickly shamble) at the first sight of anyone with a camera.

LETHALITY: All empirical data points to the conclusion that not only are these creatures harmless, but fearful of man to extreme measures. There seems to be little to worry about if one comes across one of these monsters in the wild. Caution is advised, however, if one sees their young present since it is a known fact that all mammals will attack if they sense their offspring are in danger.

WEAKNESSES: Merely humanoid, it is likely they could suffer any wound a normal man could.

POWERS: Great strength, ninja-like ability to hide from humanity.

large cranium, but not much in there

contemplative beast, always questioning his purpose in life

| First Appearance: *Harry and the Hendersons* (1987) | Endorsements: National Park Service |
| Relatives: Plenty, but good luck finding them | Description: Brown, bearded primate |

Height: 1-3 stories	Family: *Scorpionida*	Habitat: Volcanoes; sports arenas
Weight: 1/2-15 tons	Origin: Mexico	Intelligence:

BLACK SCORPION

Black scorpions were released from the dawn of time after the eruption of a Mexican volcano in 1957. Killing only at night, they come out one at a time at first, then in greater and greater hordes. Local authorities think to drop a mountain on the monsters, but one, the biggest of all, escapes. This giant insect is finally lured into a soccer stadium by the smell of blood, where it is then electrocuted. But who knows where it laid its eggs!

hairy black tentacles

large, house-sized head

BEHAVIOR: Nocturnal raids on local farms and homes for anything warm-blooded is a favorite pastime. These creatures seem to enjoy both the trampling and ripping apart of humans, as well as slurping down their thick, warm blood.

LETHALITY: Just as nasty and dangerous as one can imagine.These are bugs who see people as Pringles chips to be stacked and snacked upon. Will kill far more food than is necessary just for the fun of it.

WEAKNESSES: Super strength, great speed thanks to extra legs, incredible powerful pincers, venom-delivering tail.

First Appearance: *The Black Scorpion* (1995)	Endorsements: In negotiations with Converse
Relatives: Any number of arachnids from warmer climates	Description: Black (duh)

Height: 2 feet at the shoulder	Family: *Canis Domesticus* (Saint Bernard)	Habitat: Suburbs
Weight: 125 pounds	Origin: California	Intelligence:

CUJO

Cujo is a cute Saint Bernard, the family pet and friend we all want. But one day he's bitten by a rabid bat, and soon afterwards, goes completely bonkers while on an outing with his owners. He is transformed by rabies into a vicious beast determined to kill anyone in his path.

BEHAVIOR: Howling, drooling, housebroken, but also ferocious and unpredictable. Bad dog!!

LETHALITY: Can rip out your throat or pass on rabies virus with deep, penetrating bites.

WEAKNESSES: Puppy love, inability to negotiate sequel contracts.

POWERS: Brute strength and sharp fangs.

the true face of evil

First Appearance: *Cujo* (1983)	Endorsements: Snoopy, Taco Bell (Chihuahua)
Relatives: Beethoven	Description: Large, drooling canine

| Height: 250-275 feet | Family: Mantis | Habitat: The sea, and temperate climates |
| Weight: 1,000 tons | Origin: Arctic Circle | Intelligence: |

DEADLY MANTIS

It happens all the time, the thawing of a giant Arctic iceberg reveals a giant praying mantis. One can only guess that it was chasing a mammoth when it tripped and fell into the icy cold water, freezing it in suspended animation. It naturally wants to attack research outposts to taste the delicacy *de jour*—scientists. Having gotten a taste for man, it heads off for warmer climates, such as amply populated New York, where it quickly realizes that in the city that never sleeps, it can eat 24 hours a day.

BEHAVIOR: Mental disorientation and issues of abandonment lead him to strike out at buildings and cars.
LETHALITY: Can't hold a gun, but makes up for it by cutting people in half, very slowly (he's nasty that way).
WEAKNESSES: Large quantities of Raid, nuclear weapons, "I Love Lucy" reruns.
POWERS: Thick-skinned. Bigness and nastinessness (look, ma, we're destroying the English language).

even its claws have teeth

star of monster truck rally

| First Appearance: *The Deadly Mantis* (1957) | Endorsements: Sony (so that it would leave Tokyo alone) |
| Relatives: None still living | Description: Large, green hopping insect |

Height: 6 feet	Family: *Arachnid*	Habitat: Gold mines
Weight: 300 pounds	Origin: Prosperity, USA	Intelligence:

EIGHT LEGGED FREAKS

A chemical spill causes hundreds of little spiders to mutate to the size of SUVs. The residents of Prosperity, an old gold mining town, must battle against these bloodthirsty eight-legged freaks of nature in order to save their beloved town. They don't want to lose their homes to a bunch of fly-eating spiders, even if they are six feet tall! Though this is an admirable attitude to have, it is not recommended. It is best to run like hell if you ever run across any one of these giant furry spiders.

BEHAVIOR: The spiders squeal like schoolgirls whenever they get hurt. When they are shot, they burst open, spilling large amounts of green gloop everywhere.
LETHALITY: Might not kill you right away. Probably cocoon you for a late night snack.
WEAKNESSES: Guns, axes, car windshields.
POWERS: Stingers, mandibles, long legs for leaping onto the backs of bike riders, and webs for cocooning their victims.

Giant spiders attack!

breath freshener

large mouth
can break
off your arm

First Appearance: *Eight Legged Freaks* (2002)	Endorsements: Dr. Leonard Kipling (arachnophobia specialist)
Relatives: Eggs galore	Description: Giant spider

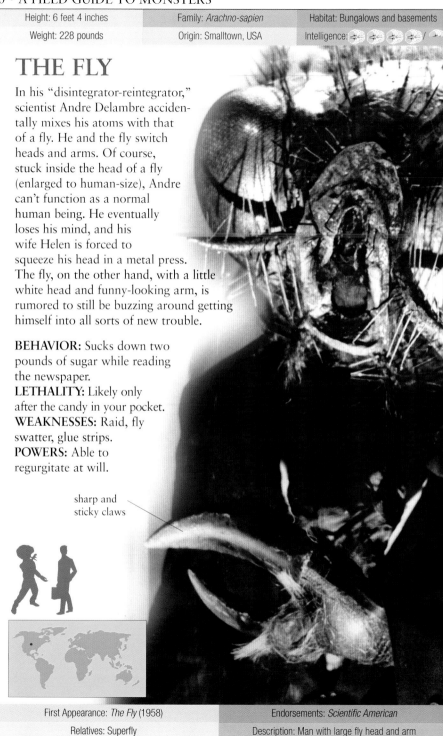

| Height: 6 feet 4 inches | Family: *Arachno-sapien* | Habitat: Bungalows and basements |
| Weight: 228 pounds | Origin: Smalltown, USA | Intelligence: |

THE FLY

In his "disintegrator-reintegrator," scientist Andre Delambre accidentally mixes his atoms with that of a fly. He and the fly switch heads and arms. Of course, stuck inside the head of a fly (enlarged to human-size), Andre can't function as a normal human being. He eventually loses his mind, and his wife Helen is forced to squeeze his head in a metal press. The fly, on the other hand, with a little white head and funny-looking arm, is rumored to still be buzzing around getting himself into all sorts of new trouble.

BEHAVIOR: Sucks down two pounds of sugar while reading the newspaper.
LETHALITY: Likely only after the candy in your pocket.
WEAKNESSES: Raid, fly swatter, glue strips.
POWERS: Able to regurgitate at will.

sharp and sticky claws

| First Appearance: *The Fly* (1958) | Endorsements: *Scientific American* |
| Relatives: Superfly | Description: Man with large fly head and arm |

Height: 6 feet 3 inches	Family: Arachno-sapien	Habitat: Laboratories
Weight: 208 pounds	Origin: Toronto	Intelligence:

BRUNDLEFLY

Known as BrundleFly, this half-fly, half-man beast (who looks a lot like the Swamp Thing or the Toxic Avenger) is a creation of an experiment gone terribly wrong. Originally he was Seth Brundle, your average ambitious young scientist, who had invented a machine that teleported bodies. But a common housefly entered the Pod with him when he was testing it out, and the machine spliced their DNA together. Now he is known to stalk around alleys and parking lots sniffing trash bins.

just wait until it grows wings

BEHAVIOR: Snapping arms of people in arm-wrestling contests (we've heard of bad losers before, but a bad winner?).

LETHALITY: Just wait until he starts throwing up on you.

WEAKNESSES: Nose, fingernails, and other parts, falling off.

POWERS: Very strong, walks on and sticks to ceilings. Just needs a theme song.

Before experiment

after experiment – big mistake...

First Appearance: *The Fly* (1986)	Endorsements: Bug-Off
Relatives: His son	Description: Fleshy green fly beast

Height: 2 feet 6 inches	Family: Winged Monkey	Habitat: Trees and evil castles
Weight: 65 pounds	Origin: Oz	Intelligence:

FLYING MONKEYS

An army of Flying Monkeys, led by chief flying monkey Nikko, is sent by the Wicked Witch of the East to capture Dorothy and her friends, the Tin Man, the Cowardly Lion, and the Scarecrow. They also make off with the dog, Toto, as well. These nightmare-inducing creatures may seem treacherous, but really it's not their fault. They really only do the Witch's bidding out of a mixture of fear and belonging. While they fear for their lives, they also know that as long as she lives, they have nowhere else to go.

feathers pulled out by toto

BEHAVIOR: Scaredy-cats by themselves, they always travel in groups.
LETHALITY: Nasty little things that swoop down on unsuspecting people and mess their hair up, or pull straw out of their limbs and carry off little pets.
WEAKNESSES: Wicked Witches.
POWERS: Ability to fly, long claws and sharp teeth.

only a wicked witch would make them wear this

Wicked Witch and Nikko

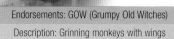

| Height: 2 feet | Family: Human | Habitat: Big tents and sideshows |
| Weight: 80 pounds | Origin: Circus | Intelligence: |

FEATHERED HEN

"Can a full-grown woman truly love a MIDGET?" Hmm, that's a tough one. But just ask the Feathered Hen, and she'll tell you that it's definitely not worth the trouble. You can find her with the FREAKS traveling carnival show. You can't miss her—she's the limbless woman covered in feathers, squawking like a chicken. Once, believe it or not, the Feathered Hen had been Cleopatra, the beautiful trapeze artist with an evil heart. She had tried to poison Hans the midget to get at his inheritance, and definitely paid the penalty after Hans' friends, other Freaks in the carnival, decided to teach her some respect.

BEHAVIOR: Can't speak or walk. Kinda wobbles around in her cage, squawking at spectators.
LETHALITY: She's so ugly that you can't look at her for more than a second.
WEAKNESSES: Greed. Midgets armed with knives.
POWERS: The evil stare.

Freak family snapshot

swollen eye

feathered tail

webbed fingers

more of a leg
man myself

now would this be a
wing or a drumstick?

| First Appearance: *Freaks* (1932) | Endorsements: Mother Goose |
| Relatives: Sideshows everywhere | Description: Limbless, feathered woman |

| Height: 2 inches | Family: *Froggus Kermitus* | Habitat: Old plantations and swamps |
| Weight: 8 ounces | Origin: Rayne, Louisiana | Intelligence: |

FROGS

A plague of lethal frogs overruns the crumbling Crockett plantation when Old Man Crocket kills a frog because he hates slimy things. Soon, the little hoppers are all over the place, determined to wipe out not only the whole family of Crocketts, but any one else who gets in their way. They're especially after those snotty princesses who refused them kisses, and, of course, the French.

BEHAVIOR: Croaking, hopping, laying 4,000 eggs at a shot, lounging in sauté pans with vino.
LETHALITY: Can make you croak. Frogs are meat eaters. The Golden Dart Frog is the most poisonous frog on Earth. Henson's Toad can beat you to death with a big schtick.
WEAKNESSES: Ammonium Nitrate is as lethal as saltwater; Cordon Bleu chefs.
POWERS: Loud noisemaking capacity, can jump twenty feet, poisonous skin.

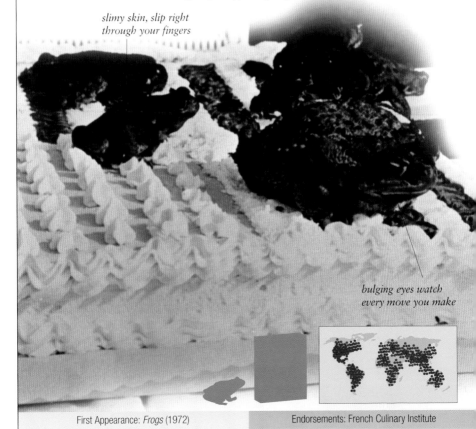

slimy skin, slip right through your fingers

bulging eyes watch every move you make

| First Appearance: *Frogs* (1972) | Endorsements: French Culinary Institute |
| Relatives: Too numerous to count | Description: Green, with warts |

Height: 5 feet 6 inches	Family: *Serpent-sapien*	Habitat: Castles and forests
Weight: 120 pounds	Origin: Vandorf, Germany	Intelligence:

GORGON

The Gorgon is out from her castle lair, turning the villagers of Vandorf into stone. Kind of a recluse, she doesn't get out much. She does enjoy the glamour of the hunt, however, chasing men through eerie gardens and surprising them in medieval castle ruins. But beware: one of her favorite pastimes is possessing unsuspecting women and turning them against their boyfriends. So if your generally sweet and caring girlfriend suddenly turns around and looks at you as if she wants to kill you, don't waste any time looking dumb and confused. Quickly get a mirror and shield yourself with it before she reveals the snakes on her head and turns you into stone.

BEHAVIOR: Does little to hide the unkempt snakes swaying about her head.
LETHALITY: Beware of her killer looks.
WEAKNESSES: Men who can't commit.
POWERS: Stone-inducing stare.

watch the eyes, or she'll turn you into stone

dangerous death-grip

First Appearance: *The Gorgon* (1964)	Endorsements: Johnson and Johnson's Snake Detangler
Relatives: Medusa	Description: Snakes on her head

| Height: 8 feet 6 inches | Family: Human |
| Weight: 500 pounds | Origin: New Mexico |

HULK

Dr. Bruce Banner is a nuclear scientist studying the effects of gamma rays on skin tissue and how they can be used to heal wounds and organs. But one of his experiments goes terribly wrong, and now when Bruce feels angry he transforms from the mild-mannered scientist into the 500-pound green monster called the HULK. Bruce may be a little moody but harmless; it's the HULK that you really must watch out for. If you ever run into him, make sure you don't step on any of his toes. And never make the mistake of calling him the "Jolly Green Giant."

hulk pissed off, you should see him when he's really angry...

the Hulk in action

BEHAVIOR: Throwing cars and tanks around like toys, leaping miles at a time, with an "I just want to be alone" attitude.
LETHALITY: Only if you really, REALLY, get him angry. Usually done by making a pass at his girlfriend Betty.
WEAKNESSES: Government officials and soldiers.
POWERS: Super human strength and near invulnerability.

First Appearance: *Hulk* (1966)
Relatives: She-Hulk

Habitat: Laboratories

Intelligence:

even his hair has muscles

this is some chip on his shoulder

Endorsements: Lycra

Description: Green muscle man

| Height: 5 feet 10 inches | Family: Human | Habitat: Boarding houses |
| Weight: 175 pounds | Origin: England | Intelligence: ⚙ ⚙ ⚙ ⚙ |

INVISIBLE MAN

Dr. Jack Griffin is a brilliant scientist that creates an elixir to make himself invisible to the naked eye. His intentions at first seem innocent enough—for the attention of a young beautiful woman. But he slowly comes to realize the full potential of his invisibility. The more he uses the potion, the more his mind becomes unhinged and he moves closer to the realm of madness (a short bus ride from insanity). His emotions transform from love into greed and malice, and he terrorizes the countryside long before anyone had heard of Donald Rumsfeld. Soon the police are onto his game and are chasing the thief and murderer. His chance to return to a normal life has gone. Though Jack is considered to have been killed by authorities, there is new intelligence that he survived this ordeal and now works for the government as an agent of the League Of Extraordinary Gentlemen.

jeepers creepers, where'd you hide those peepers?

BEHAVIOR: Wraps himself in bandages, wears a trench coat and sunglasses in all weather.
LETHALITY: Unfeeling and cruel. Little regard for human life.
WEAKNESSES: Can't go out invisible with a full stomach.
POWERS: Er...invisibility...

Height: 8 feet	Family: Robot	Habitat: Ships
Weight: 5 tons	Origin: Greece	Intelligence:

MINOTAUR

Minotaur is a mechanical beast made by the evil witch Zenobia and her son Raffi to battle Sinbad the sailor. Raffi fashioned a mechanical heart made out of gold, which Zenobia placed inside a bronze statue of the Minotaur, with the head of a bull and the body of a man. When it comes to life, she names it Minaton and orders it to power a mechanical ship by turning a crank that sets in motion six pairs of oars, and then sets off in pursuit of Sinbad, who has sailed off with Princess Farah and Kassim. With no real mind of its own, the Minotaur is still employed as the lethal henchman of the evil witch.

bronze snout

cherished gold medallion

BEHAVIOR: Creaks a lot as he moves. Likes to row ships for days on end.
LETHALITY: IF he can catch you, you're in deep doo-doo.
WEAKNESSES: Rusts in water. Large rocks.
POWERS: Very strong. Rows really fast, moves very slow.

First Appearance: *Sinbad and the Eye of the Tiger* (1977)	Endorsements: 3-in-1 Oil
Relatives: Iron Giant	Description: Bronze bull-headed robot

Height: 6 feet 5 inches	Family: Homicidal Maniac	Habitat: Camps
Weight: 300 pounds	Origin: Crystal Lake	Intelligence:

JASON VOORHEES

A 300-pound unstoppable killing machine, you can recognize Jason Voorhees by his trademark, white hockey mask. Killed in 1957 when he drowned at Camp Crystal Lake, Jason has been coming back from the dead to get his revenge on the camp. He seems to have a real problem letting go of things. It turns out that Jason was a deformed little boy who was ridiculed by both camp-goers and counselors. He died while the two counselors who should have been watching him were having sex. And now, decades after the fact, he lurks in dark corners, preying upon horny teenagers.

merchandizing on the mask alone has made him a multi-millionaire

BEHAVIOR: Chops and hacks up teenage camp counselors by the dozen.
LETHALITY: Completely deadly. Has no compassion, will kill anything on sight.
WEAKNESSES: Stupidity and his love for his mommy.
POWERS: Swings a mean machete.

that isn't his blood

he takes this to bed with him

First Appearance: *Friday the 13th* (1980)	Endorsements: All Best Hockey equipment
Relatives: Mother recently deceased	Description: Deranged psycho in hockey mask

| Height: 6 feet | Family: Homicidal Maniac | Habitat: Mental institutions |
| Weight: 200 pounds | Origin: Haddonfield, USA | Intelligence: |

MICHAEL MYERS

Not to be confused with Jason Voorhees, who hides his face behind a hockey mask, Michael Myers is more for the theatrics and prefers a white stage mask when prowling for horny teenagers. A killer since the age of six, Michael is pure evil, and continually returns to his hometown of Haddonfield to terrorize the new inhabitants of his childhood house. Like Jason, he also hates sexual promiscuity and goes quite crazy with a butcher's knife.

BEHAVIOR: Leaps out of closets and hacks people to bits.
LETHALITY: Unstoppable.
WEAKNESSES: Not sure if he has one...Bit of a prude.
POWERS: Seemingly indestructible.

big "star trek" fan, models himself on "data"

kitchen butcher knife

Here's Michael, screwing on his mask

| First Appearance: *Halloween* (1978) | Endorsements: Moral Minority |
| Relatives: Jason Voorhees, Dick Cheney | Description: Serial killer with white mask |

| Height: 20 feet | Family: Gorilla | Habitat: Jungles |
| Weight: 400 pounds | Origin: Africa | Intelligence: |

MIGHTY JOE YOUNG

In Hollywood, Joe, the gorilla, first appears in a nightclub with his owner and friend, Jill, playing the piano. It's one class act and Joe is a success. However, it doesn't take long for movie producers to find a way to exploit the amicable gorilla, and soon he's signed a big-deal Hollywood contract. Jill and Joe both realize that Hollywood-life isn't for them; but when Joe escapes, he causes havoc around the city. Fortunately, there are children trapped inside a burning orphanage for him to save, and Joe becomes a bonafide hero. Now he's back on the nightclub circuit, reaping the benefits of being everyone's lovable gorilla.

that's a guilty look if ever i saw one

likes to show off his biceps

BEHAVIOR: Will do anything to please his friends.
LETHALITY: Does not intentionally hurt people.
WEAKNESSES: Pure and innocent. Easily exploited.
POWERS: Great strength and stamina.

hairy palms

| First Appearance: *Mighty Joe Young* (1949) | Endorsements: Sierra Club |
| Relatives: George of the Jungle | Description: Singing primate |

Height: 50 feet	Family: *Bigicus Apicus*	Habitat: Steamy, sweaty jungle
Weight: Several tons	Origin: Skull Island	Intelligence:

KING KONG

A giant 50-foot ape, which the natives call Kong, gets drugged, kidnapped, and taken to New York City. Suddenly, he's thrown into a low-budget Hollywood picture without a script (that would mean options and fees), but a lot of publicity engagements. One day, he just can't take being exploited like this any longer. He escapes out of his cage, flattens the audience, and runs amok in the city, taking the lead actress with him. Unfortunately, the date goes bad when the Air Force show up. Now working on a tight schedule, he's usually under lock and key. But occasionally, Kong breaks out and exhibits classic Hollywood-actor behavior around town…you know, fondling girls, trashing hotel rooms, and hanging from tall buildings.

BEHAVIOR: Beats chest, picks his nose, eats a lot.

ferocious scream

LETHALITY:
His big foot squashes heads. He'd kill a hundred or so just sitting down. Kills thousands using Madison Square Garden as a bathroom.
WEAKNESSES: Berry juice and blondes, brunettes, redheads…
POWERS: Very strong. Watch out for when he falls over.

chiseled chest

First Appearance: *King Kong* (1933)	Endorsements: Hair loss, Viagra
Relatives: Son of Kong! What did happen to Fay Wray?	Description: Giant dominant ape

Height: 5 feet 6 inches	Family: *Homo Erectus*	Habitat: Burrows and caves
Weight: Approximately 185 pounds	Origin: England	Intelligence:

MORLOCKS

Morlocks were once human, but with the advent of continuing warfare, they had decided that life would be better underground in the cold and dark caverns. They eventually devolved into subterranean, ape-like monsters who cannot tolerate sunlight. Food isn't plentiful underground and being human (or sub-human), a diet of roots and grubs is just not practical. So there is a desperate search for meat. And the only nearby source, besides feeding on themselves, is above ground. So beware: Morlocks will do anything to lure surface dwellers underground.

homecoming king

BEHAVIOR: Tend to lurch around on all fours.
LETHALITY: Body odor not withstanding, they are very strong and can bite through bone.

homecoming queen

WEAKNESSES: Light and Old Spice cologne.
POWERS: Night vision, excellent hearing, and sharp pointy teeth.

First Appearance: *The Time Machine* (1960)	Endorsements: Saddam Hussein and Osama bin Laden
Relatives: They have been known to play with their food	Description: Cannibal with shaggy hair

| Length: 180 feet | Family: *Mosura* | Habitat: Jungle |
| Weight: 20,000 tons | Origin: Beiru | Intelligence: |

MOTHRA

Gigantic moth-goddess, known as Mothra, loves more than anything else the enigmatic singing of two tiny twin princesses (each a foot tall). Worshipped on the small island of Beiru, Mothra's idyllic life gets interrupted when explorer and scientist Clark Nelson abducts the princesses for his vaudeville show. But their serene, bewitching singing serves as a telepathic SOS to Mothra, who looks for the women in Tokyo, causing the usual havoc and mayhem.

BEHAVIOR: Loves listening to the singing princesses.
LETHALITY: Take away the singing princesses and she'll kill millions and trample an entire city.
WEAKNESSES: Singing princesses.
POWERS: You name it, she can do it: flies at Mach 3; gives off poisonous yellow dust; emits rays from antennae; discharges bolts of lightning from wings; can block Godzilla's radioactive breath ray; and she's even telepathic.

giant aviator eyes

building-crushing wings

| First Appearance: *Mothra (Mosura)* (1961) | Endorsements: The Cosmos |
| Relatives: Larva in waiting | Description: Giant wings, large bug eyes |

| Height: 6 feet 1 inch | Family: Ogre | Habitat: Swamps and bogs |
| Weight: 400 pounds | Origin: The Swamp | Intelligence: |

SHREK

Shrek is a large, green ogre, who lives in a swamp outside of the magical kingdom of Duloc. Once known as a brutal, smelly monster feared and reviled by all, Shrek has become quite the ladies' man since meeting his new bride Fiona. For one thing, he's showering regularly now, and he doesn't tear the heads off of everything in sight anymore. But don't accuse him of going soft to his face, or else he'll smash you with his club.

BEHAVIOR: Grumpy, keeps to himself. Loves his privacy and will go to any lengths to keep it.

LETHALITY: Don't go down wind of this ogre.

WEAKNESSES: Under that gruff exterior lies a heart of gold (well maybe gold is too strong a word).

POWERS: Very strong, farts that can kill from twenty paces (fish anyway), and extremely stubborn (Shrek has actually turned that into a power).

| First Appearance: *Shrek* (2001) | Endorsements: Everything under the sun |
| Relatives: Fungus the Bogeyman | Description: Green and smelly |

Height: 5 feet 10 inches	Family: Mad scientist	Habitat: Strip clubs
Weight: 185 pounds	Origin: Rome	Intelligence: 

PROFESSOR ALBERTO LEVIN

Scientist Alberto Levin has developed a treatment that helps restore the face of a stripper, who had been disfigured in an accident. Levin ends up falling in love with her, and to keep her beautiful, he gives her additional treatments using the glands of murdered women. He uses another treatment on himself to disguise himself while he is shopping for victims (or is that "chopping"?)—a serum that disfigures him beyond recognition.

BEHAVIOR: Haunts strip clubs and other gentlemen's establishments.
LETHALITY: Only if you're a buxom young stripper with all your glands intact.
WEAKNESSES: As above…
POWERS: Armed with a serum that can change him from prince to beast.

upset she won't play 'beauty and the beast'

tired of the lap dances

First Appearance: *Atom Age Vampire* (1960)	Endorsements: Donor Cards
Relatives: Nutty professor	Description: Mutant with reptile skin

| Height: 5 feet 5 inches | Family: Hunchback | Habitat: Cathedrals |
| Weight: 185 pounds | Origin: Paris, France | Intelligence: |

QUASIMODO

Quasimodo, despite his grotesque appearance, is exceptionally agile as he moves through the Cathedral and out onto its roof. Showing no fear for its height, climbing down its façade, he swings down and takes his friend Esmeralda, the beautiful gypsy dancer, into the Cathedral where she will be safe within the its wall. Quasimodo leaps onto "Big Louise" (his favorite "Belle") and rides his beloved huge chime back and forth sending its mighty sound throughout Paris for his beloved Esmeralda.

Esmerelda and Quasimodo

BEHAVIOR: Shy and reserved. Likes swinging from ropes.
LETHALITY: Only if you threaten Esmeralda.
WEAKNESSES: Hates noise, people, and crowded places.
POWERS: Did we mention the swinging already?

| First Appearance: *Hunchback of Notre Dame* (1923) | Endorsements: Liberty Bell makers |
| Relative: Igor | Description: Short hunchback |

| Height: 2 inches | Family: *Hymenoptera* | Habitat: Gardens |
| Weight: Tiny | Origin: Africa | Intelligence: |

SAVAGE BEES

For years, scientists have been warning that killer bees from Africa have been breeding with the gentler bees of more northern climes and that they will slowly extend their territory northward. Entomologist Brad Crane is the first to discover that something is making these bees come together in huge, killer swarms. Don't underestimate the effectiveness of these bees. When they first appeared on the scene, they attacked Texas, blowing up nuclear plants and setting fire to Houston. Capable of incredible things, they can bring down helicopters and derail trains.

BEHAVIOR: Dour and miserable, will commit suicide over anything.
LETHALITY: Only in mass.
WEAKNESSES: Insecticide
POWERS: Stingers

| First Appearance: *The Swarm* (1978) | Endorsements: Honey Nut Cheerios |
| Relatives: Larvae everywhere | Description: Black and yellow |

Height: 9 feet	Family: Wendigo	Habitat: Caves
Weight: 300-400 pounds	Origin: North America	Intelligence: 

SASQUATCH

Sasquatch was originally thought to have been the same family as the Yeti or Big Foot. But since the release of The Untold story, both Big Foot and Yeti have denied any association with the Sasquatch family. Who or what the Sasquatch really is unsure; we're sure the truth is out there somewhere (probably in FBI agent Mulder's burnt files). But what is sure is that the Sasquatch is very concerned about the future of the planet, and is currently rumored to moonlight for PETA.

desperate need of a dentist

BEHAVIOR: Likes to spy on people and is quite the voyeur. Fishes through garbage cans.

LETHALITY: Normally he is probably quite docile, but get him on a subject like the environment and he's a killing machine. Someone give him a map to the Republican-led EPA.

WEAKNESSES: Less hair than its Yeti and Big Foot relatives, it must move around a lot to keep warm. Pulling apart helpless scientists can provide a good work out.

POWERS: Ability to hide from mankind for centuries despite not being able to see properly.

First Appearance: *The Untold* (2002)	Endorsements: Rogaine Hair Restorer
Relatives: Yeah, but none that will ever admit it	Description: Hairy beast with long fangs

Height: 6 feet 4 1/2 inches	Family: Dead	Habitat: Desert
Weight: 255 pounds	Origin: Egypt	Intelligence:

SCORPION KING

The Scorpion King is the commander of the Army of Anubis (who just happens to be the God of the Dead). Originally known as Mathayus, the evil leader of the Akkadians, the Scorpion King sold his soul to Anubis so that he could return from the dead to avenge the defeat of his fallen army. With his soul locked in an oasis in the desert, this monster is quite the ruthless beast. To rule the world, he'll stop at nothing.

spends a lot of time in the gym

BEHAVIOR: Single-minded in his desire to kill all those that trespass in the temple, he stings a lot. Grunts too.

LETHALITY: Watch out for his pinchers and watch for his tail, stings a lot. His teeth may LOOK white, but watch out for his breath (even Scope can't keep a mouth smelling sweet after several thousand years locked in a pyramid).

WEAKNESSES: Quick to lose temper; lousy at knitting; spears through chests.

POWERS: Opening cans and jars. Did we mention stings?

First Appearance: *The Mummy Returns* (2001)

Relatives: None that he kept track of

Endorsements: SWF (Sumerian Wrestling Federation)

Description: Well-tanned pro-wrestler

| Height: 50 feet | Family: Human | Habitat: Desert |
| Weight: 5 tons | Origin: New Mexico | Intelligence: |

50 FOOT WOMAN

Alcoholic heiress Nancy Archer discovers a UFO, and inside, there is a forty-foot bald alien. Unknown to both, he accidentally alters her genetic make-up. Before long, Nancy discovers that she is starting to grow and eventually, she has reached 50 feet. Her new body takes a huge toll on her mental well-being. When she realizes that she won't ever be normal again, she does what any wife would do, she blames it on the husband. But before getting her revenge on her cheating husband, she first must see what fashions are available in her new fifty-foot size. Bed sheets seem to be the new fad and she's always checking out new merchandise at the department store.

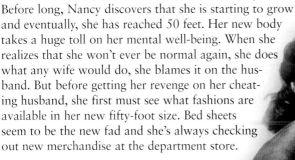

treats men like toys

BEHAVIOR: Constant frustration at not being able to get the latest fashions in her size.
LETHALITY: Husbands beware. She'll squeeze you to death.
WEAKNESSES: Body and brain can't keep up with rapid increase in size.
POWERS: Big mouth, big feet and big hands (all the better to crush hubby with).

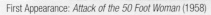

First Appearance: *Attack of the 50 Foot Woman* (1958)
Relatives: The Amazing Colossal Man

Endorsements: Big and Beautiful Fashions
Description: Brunette with long, long legs

Height: 60 feet	Family: Sphecoidea	Habitat: Board rooms, bedrooms, hives
Weight: 108 pounds	Origin: Congo	Intelligence:

TARANTULA

This 60-foot gargantuan arachnid is the result of yet another experiment gone terribly wrong. The tarantula had been injected with a special growth-inducing formula by incompetent scientists who brilliantly succeeded in injecting themselves with the formula (and then dying from it a few days later). The tarantula, of course, escapes its cage and grows even larger. It has been loose in the country, attacking not only people, but cattle herds as well.

all he wants is a fly

BEHAVIOR: Eats men and cattle. Chirps like a bird. Likes to look in windows as people are undressing.

LETHALITY: Sixty feet of meat eating, goo-spewing, tarantula—Lethal? You need to ask?

WEAKNESSES: Napalm

POWERS: Stinger, mandibles, startling appearance

split ends

First Appearance: *Tarantula* (1955)	Endorsements: Goodyear
Relatives: Spiderman	Description: Black and hairy

| Height: Unknown | Family: Alien | Habitat: Men and dogs |
| Weight: Unknown | Origin: Antarctic | Intelligence: |

THE THING

An alien life-form, the Thing is a shape-changing monster that can assume the identity of anything that it kills. It was first discovered in the frozen wastelands of the Antarctic by a group of scientists who made the mistake of taking pity on a seemingly harmless dog. But during the night, the dog mutates and morphs into a series of increasingly twisted and grotesque monsters, attacking dogs and humans alike. Since this first encounter, the Thing has successfully infiltrated other continents, including North America. Unfortunately, it has become almost impossible to tell who has been infected and who hasn't.

BEHAVIOR: Hides inside animal tissue like a parasite.
LETHALITY: Once infected, you're dead and your body belongs to the Thing.
WEAKNESSES: Cold and extreme heat.
POWERS: Can change shape, but is always ugly.

eye infection

First Appearance: *The Thing* (1982)

Relatives: The Hidden

Endorsements: The Seal Clubbers Need Love Too Society

Description: Parasite

| Height: 6 feet 6 inches | Family: Human | Habitat: Space capsules |
| Weight: 210 pounds | Origin: Earth | Intelligence: |

THE INCREDIBLE MELTING MAN

Apparently, looking through the rings of Saturn somehow caused astronaut Steve West to start melting—hence, the Incredible Melting Man. On returning to Earth, after having traveled the solar system for a couple of years, the Incredible Melting Man has a terrible habit of eating people. Prime delicacies for this six-foot pile of melting gloop: people in the medical profession.

BEHAVIOR: Drips on the carpets, attacks nurses, eats victims.
LETHALITY: It's you or him, baby, and he isn't about to let it be him.
WEAKNESSES: Loses several pounds every time he changes his clothes.
POWERS: Can suck flesh off your bones. Gets stronger as he melts.

skin melting off

| First Appearance: *The Incredible Melting Man* (1977) | Endorsements: Pizza Hut |
| Relatives: Four cheese pizza | Description: Skin looks like brains |

| Height: 6 feet, 5 feet, 4 feet . . . | Family: Human | Habitat: Basements |
| Weight: 180 pounds, 179 pounds. . . | Origin: America | Intelligence: |

THE INCREDIBLE SHRINKING MAN

Growing smaller by the minute, it is hard to detect the Incredible Shrinking Man with the naked eye. Once, he used to be all-American boy Scott Carey, but started shrinking after getting stuck in some fog while in his boat on the river. The doctors have been unable to offer him any advice or help. Soon, he will shrink to be nothing but a speck of dust in your eye. But, be careful—he may be microscopic, but he's got a nasty temper.

BEHAVIOR: Gets through clothes faster than the average teen. Verbally bites the heads off everyone who cares.
Very frustrated.
LETHALITY: Only if you're an insect.

WEAKNESSES: Cats, spiders, mice, birds, people, etc…
POWERS: Brains! There isn't anything else going for him.

| First Appearance: *The Incredible Shrinking Man* (1957) | Endorsements: United States National Deficit |
| Relatives: The Incredible Shrinking Woman | Description: Small man |

Height: 5 feet 6 inches	Family: *Sphecoidea*	Habitat: Board rooms, bedrooms, hives
Weight: 108 pounds	Origin: North America	Intelligence:

WASP WOMAN

The head of a cosmetics firm, getting on in years but still vain as a school girl, authorizes the production of a wrinkle cream made from wasp enzymes. She uses it on herself and soon she's as beautiful as ever. One little annoying problem, however, the creme causes her to occasionally transform into some sort of mutant insect thing that needs to kill, kill, kill! And you thought throwing up dinner was a long way to go for glamor.

BEHAVIOR: Throwing hissy fits, moaning about fading beauty, killing over and over for temporary good looks.

LETHALITY: Somewhat lethal, but in the strict vampire sense of killing for nourishment. Killer good looks, though.

WEAKNESSES: Raid, fly swatter, glue strips

POWERS: Stinger, mandibles, startling appearance

honey-producing bee with giant female head

and this was just breakfast

First Appearance: *The Wasp Woman* (1960)	Endorsements: Republican National Committee
Relatives: Larvae everywhere	Description: Big and bugly

MUTATED VEGETABLES

For centuries now, man has been concerned that the ecosystem is one day going to strike back at us. We know the damage we have done and are continuing to do, all in the name of progress and disposable diapers, and many believe that mankind has proven itself unfit to hold the responsibility of safeguarding the planet for future generations. That judgment seems to be upheld by nature itself.

While this section is a small one, there are more and more cases being report-ed of attacks by trees and plants. n every instance, the vegetation in question has cited the Fifth Amendment. With only unsubstantiated allegations to go on, and no witnesses to interview, there just isn't a case. You can't bring a tree in for questioning or lock up some shrubbery overnight.

The lack of subjects in this section only shows that we are not looking into this seriously enough. With real detective work, many more cases would come to light, but how far can we go? As the pollen count continues to rise at an alarming rate each year, do we start locking up plants for deliberately overpro-ducing pollen, knowing that as the count goes up, a greater number of us will be affected?

Some fear that the plant life of the earth will say "Enough!" and turn against us. But we know that the ecosystem has already moved waaaay past that point. Make no mistake, it may sound crazy until you pause and consider the evidence, the Earth has declared war on man, we just haven't listened to the message.

Height: 11 feet	Family: *Dionæa Muscipula*	Habitat: Large earthenware containers
Weight: 2 tons (including container)	Origin: Uncertain	Intelligence:

AUDREY II

Giant alien plant named Audrey II has a bad craving for human flesh. Named by its owner, Seymour Krelborn (neighborhood florist nerd), for his secret crush, Audrey II is one manipulative diva, who uses Seymour's infatuation as a way to procure her meals. She can't stand competition and even wants to feast on her namesake. Beware, she'll gobble you up whole and enjoy every second of it.

BEHAVIOR: Sits in her pot and waits for warm-blooded creatures to walk by. Reported to be perfectly willing to be fed her fill of blood in a quite docile fashion if sufficient quantities are provided. Will snag a Type O snack anyway she can.

extra-thick vines will strange you to death

sings while she eats

LETHALITY: Quite lethal to both man and beast. She doesn't discriminate—as long as there are red corpuscles to consume.

WEAKNESSES: Cold weather, Weed-B-Gone. Well-drained soil.

POWERS: Massive teeth, extensive tentacle-like vine system, great strength.

First Appearance: *The Little Shop of Horrors* (1960)	Endorsements: InterFlora
Relatives: The Thing From Another World (cousin)	Appearance: Female plant with big, luscious lips

Height: Varies, 2 inches-4 feet	Family: *Lycopersicon Esculentum*	Habitat: Fields, gardens, salads
Weight: Varies, 3 ounces-90 pounds	Origin: One backyard or another	Intelligence:

KILLER TOMATOES

Many make the mistake of laughing off the seriousness of these killer mutant tomatoes. Hey, they're just tomatoes right? Wrong. They're not just tomatoes, but vicious killing machines with insatiable appetites for destruction. They love terrorizing the innocent, and pull such deadly antics like sneaking up on swimmers, stealing cars, and running down pedestrians.

BEHAVIOR: Simply the most hostile vegetable force ever seen. Make Venus FlyTraps seem like Shrinking Violets. Will attack anything that moves and sauce it to death.

LETHALITY: Surprisingly deadly for a fruit. Varied sizes and willingness to hunt in packs make them dangerous customers. It has been theorized that they target vegans in particular, but this has yet to be proved.

WEAKNESSES: Lack of sunlight, ketchup-bottling factories.

POWERS: Can bounce and roll at high speeds without bruising. Willing to throw themselves at their prey repeatedly until they have pummeled their opponent into submission or themselves into spaghetti sauce.

sweating ketchup

all that genetic modification had to have an effect eventually

First Appearance: *Attack of the Killer Tomatoes* (1978)	Endorsements: Chef Boy-Ar-Dee
Relatives: Mr. Potato Head (in-law)	Description: Red, round, and juicy

Length: 5-6 feet	Family: *Pisum sativum*
Weight: 5-10 pounds	Origin: Not of our world

PODS

These bizarre interstellar travelers came to Earth with the thought of not so much taking over, but fitting in. They have attempted numerous times to replace the human race with their own hive-mind replicates. Watching the activities of various groups, from the Moonies to the Democratic Party, has convinced many that this threat has yet to be eradicated from the planet.

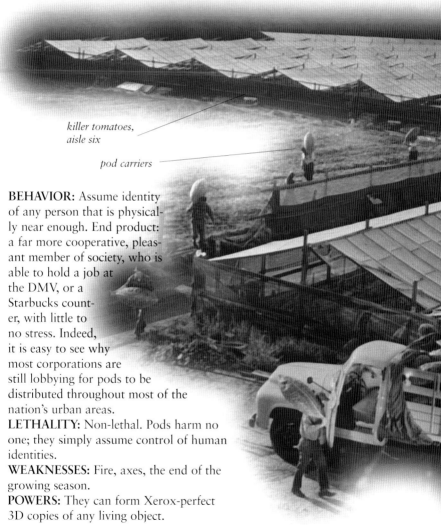

killer tomatoes, aisle six

pod carriers

BEHAVIOR: Assume identity of any person that is physically near enough. End product: a far more cooperative, pleasant member of society, who is able to hold a job at the DMV, or a Starbucks counter, with little to no stress. Indeed, it is easy to see why most corporations are still lobbying for pods to be distributed throughout most of the nation's urban areas.

LETHALITY: Non-lethal. Pods harm no one; they simply assume control of human identities.

WEAKNESSES: Fire, axes, the end of the growing season.

POWERS: They can form Xerox-perfect 3D copies of any living object.

First Appearance: *Invasion of the Body Snatchers* (1956)

Relatives: Everyone in sight

Habitat: Basements, attics, and the backs of trucks

Intelligence:

*union-certified
pod handler*

harvested pods

Endorsements: Hewlett Packard

Description: Green vegetation

Height: 9 feet	Family: Human/Vegetation	Habitat: The Green
Weight: 340 pounds	Origin: North America	Intelligence:

SWAMP THING

Swamp Thing is a walking morass of vines and vegetation with the ability to walk and talk. Before the mutation, however, he was Doctor Alec Holland, who tragically fell into the swamp when his lab exploded, causing his charred remains to mix with the chemicals from his experiments. When water from the swamp added into this toxic mix, the transformation was complete. Now, he remains hidden from the outside world, fighting social injustice behind the scenes.

BEHAVIOR: Wanders the swamps and bayous, looking for evil to thwart or beautiful women to protect and lust after. Hates city life.

LETHALITY: The Swamp Thing is an extremely lethal creature, but it only displays violence toward evils approved by the Liberal Left.

WEAKNESSES: DDT, root rot, and Communism.

POWERS: Can communicate with plants and duplicate any of their abilities or characteristics; i.e., grow thorns, strangle with vines, become airborne as a seedling, et cetera.

First Appearance: *Swamp Thing* (1982)	Endorsements: Miracle-Gro
Relatives: Every leaf and twig	Description: Walking broccoli stalk

Height: 4-15 feet	Family: Unknown	Habitat: Anywhere away from saltwater
Weight: 2-65 pounds	Origin: Meteor shower	Intelligence:

TRIFFIDS

These interstellar cucumbers traveled to Earth hitching a ride on a meteor shower. While the astrological phenomenon had the effect of leaving most of the planet's population blind, the seedlings took root and then made their bid to take over. Soulless killers, they have absolutely no qualms about taking advantage of the blind.

BEHAVIOR: Soaking up sun and blood. Triffids tend to act like normal plants until they reach maturity, at which point they uproot themselves and start larking about looking for the sightless to serve as lunchmeats.

LETHALITY: Extremely lethal. These voracious veggies have only one thing on their fertilized minds, and that's slaughtering every human in sight. These are extraordinarily hostile creatures and should be avoided at all costs.

WEAKNESSES: Saltwater, weed whackers.

POWERS: Mobility (unusual in plants), strangling vines with enormous crushing power.

doesn't handle rejection very well

First Appearance: *Day of the Triffids* (1962)	Endorsements: Harry's Instant Gardens
Relatives: Pods	Description: Large walking plant

MONSTER MEN

Human Nature. Many have come to the realization that when you put these two words together, you have an oxymoron. Two opposites. When we read reports about a vampire or werewolf killing some young coed, not even out of her teens, we feel horror and rage against the perpetrators of such a vile act. We want them wiped out of existence, never once stopping to question—Was this really such an inhuman act? Is man better than these beasts or have we just done too good of a job fooling ourselves?

It is also interesting to note that the first five entries are Doctors. Scientists do have an uncanny way of standing back from society and looking at the rest of us like white mice in a maze. Some may argue that this sort of behavior is just as disturbing as the vampire who watches its prey. They both see themselves as superior and that their ideals are far above our rights or desires for a normal life. We have become cattle or sheep in their eyes, and we all know what happens to cattle and sheep.

We all go down better with a nice glass of Chianti.

| Height: 5 feet 11 inches | Family: Human | Habitat: Hotels and axe shops |
| Weight: 170 pounds | Origin: Colorado | Intelligence: |

JACK TORRANCE

Jack Torrance is a struggling author currently suffering from writers' block. Under enough pressure as it is, he becomes susceptible to ghosts and comes under their evil control. While taking a job as the caretaker of the huge Overlook Hotel in Colorado, which closes for the winter every year, Jack completely loses it and starts attacking his family. It is rumored that Jack has given up writing completely, choosing instead the life of an evil ghost. He has taken up permanent residence in the attic of the Overlook Hotel, and can be heard at night, sledgehammering his way through walls.

BEHAVIOR: Talks to himself, walks around hotel lobbies at night, puts axes through doors. Terrorizes others when stuck on a chapter.
LETHALITY: Will kill anyone in his way.
WEAKNESSES: Purely flesh and blood hang-ups.
POWERS: Able to switch from meek book writer to axe-wielding maniac with ease.

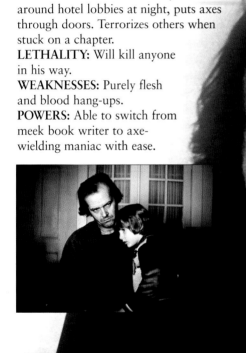

| First Appearance: *The Shining (1980)* | Endorsements: Marriott Hotels |
| Relatives: Tony Blair | Description: Psycho |

Height: 6 feet 1 inch	Family: Supervillain	Habitat: Comic book stores
Weight: 160 pounds	Origin: Long Island	Intelligence:

MR. GLASS

Elijah Price (otherwise known as "Mr. Glass") is determined to be the ultimate comic book villain because he believes that this is who he was meant to be. Born with osteogenesis imperfecta, a condition that leaves the bones extremely brittle, Mr. Glass was so fragile that the mere act of birth had shattered most of his bones. Growing up, his only comfort was reading comic books. As he studied and pored over these four-color gems of escapism, he compared himself to the costumed characters within and eventually found an association that would direct the rest of his life. But every villain needs a hero to fight, right? If there was someone like him who was so weak, Mr. Glass decided that there must be someone who is his exact opposite. Where he is weak, that person would be strong. Where his bones would break with ease, that person's bones would be unbreakable. Mr. Glass found his opposite in David Dunn, who somehow survives a train disaster without a scratch. Thanks to Mr. Glass, David eventually realizes his potential and becomes a hero. And now, Mr. Glass can take his place as the supervillain.

BEHAVIOR: Does everything with extreme care so as not to hurt himself. Spends a lot of time in a wheelchair as his bones break very easily. Morally reprehensible.

comic book, his bible

weak bones easily broken

LETHALITY: Has no concept of remorse and will kill innocent women and children to prove his point.
WEAKNESSES: His bones are extremely fragile.
POWERS: His strength lies in what he is capable of and what he will do to achieve his desires.

First Appearance: *Unbreakable* (2000)	Endorsements: Osborn Corporation
Relatives: Joker, Green Goblin	Description: Feeble man

| Height: 5 feet 9 inches | Family: Human | Habitat: Cities and dreams |
| Weight: 265 pounds | Origin: Germany | Intelligence: |

DOCTOR CALIGARI

Head doctor of sanitarium by day, and a sideshow performer by night, Caligari is a demonic, murderous doctor. He thinks himself untouchable by all, including the authorities. Dr. Caligari uses as his weapon a young man, whom he controls through dreams. The young man is unable to wake up from his coma, and therefore, at the evil doctor's disposal to commit any sin he asks of him, in what he thinks is a dream. But the doctor's plans are foiled when the young man's girlfriend suspects Caligari responsible for her boyfriend's death.

never leaves his house without his tall hat

BEHAVIOR: Caligari disguises himself by gelling his white hair, wearing a tall hat, and acting wildly (if Clark Kent can get away with just a pair of glasses…).

LETHALITY: Caligari is not a man excited by riches, nor is he after world domination; his position at the asylum is all the power he needs. But this makes him all the more dangerous. He just cares about the experiment and its results.

WEAKNESSES: Superiority and overconfidence that keep him from seeing straight.

POWERS: To fool the minds of the young and twist the dreams of the innocent.

The Doctor and his coma patient

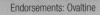

Height: 5 feet 6 inches	Family: Human	Habitat: Sparely equipped labs
Weight: 145 pounds	Origin: Peru	Intelligence: ⊝ ⊝ ⊝ ⊶

DR. CYCLOPS

Dr. Thorkel (otherwise known as Dr. Cyclops) invites a number of scientists to join him in his work. He then proceeds to turn his experimental shrinking ray on them, reducing them and several locals to the size of dolls. Unfortunately, he ends up having to chase them about relentlessly afterwards, unable to capture them because of their size.

BEHAVIOR: With the obviously insane Dr. Cyclops, anything is possible. As likely to greet one with a pleasant "hello" as he is to try and scoop them up in a butterfly net.

LETHALITY: Not very. Inept at mayhem, Dr. Cyclops is a fairly harmless individual, as monsters go. Though he has no compunctions over slaughtering innocents, he simply doesn't have the skills to pull it off.

WEAKNESSES: Limited vision, puny even for a mere human.

POWERS: Brainpower to invent shrinking ray.

sore eyes

sight for...

First Appearance: *Dr. Cyclops* (1940)	Endorsements: Visine
Relatives: Dr. Freeze	Description: Bald with glasses

Height: 5 feet 10 inches	Family: Human	Habitat: Black & white castles
Weight: 158 pounds	Origin: Eastern Europe	Intelligence:

DR. VICTOR FRANKENSTEIN

Rejected by the polite scientific community of his time, Victor Frankenstein resorts to grave robbing to collect the necessary parts for his grand experiment—reanimating lifeless tissue. His attempt to impersonate the Almighty produces one misshapen humanoid creature, most often incorrectly referred to by the illiterate as "Frankenstein," as if it had created itself.

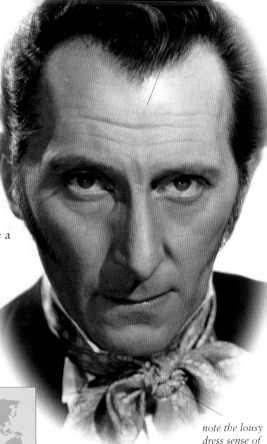

note the high forehead of the evil genius

BEHAVIOR: Perfectly willing to turn his back on morality and human decency at a moment's notice for the chance to stitch together some rotting body parts into a hulking zombie. Operates with the ethical restraint of a Borgia or even a Clinton.

LETHALITY: Frankenstein is not exactly lethal himself, but his creations have proved to be powerfully destructive. Though his first monster was reasonably harmless, his later efforts proved to be Earth-shattering.

WEAKNESSES: Broods a lot, given to fits of melancholy and nostalgia.

POWERS: Can create life as easily as most people can create a tuna melt.

"Wow, can we do that again?"

note the lousy dress sense of the evil genius

First Appearance: *Frankenstein* (1931)	Endorsements: Universal Studios
Relatives: His Monster, Bride of Frankenstein, Jesse Helms	Description: Mad Scientist

Height: 5 feet 6 inches/6 feet 4 inches	Family: Human	Habitat: Laboratories/Cheap bars
Weight: 135 pounds/395 pounds	Origin: England	Intelligence:

DR. JEKYLL/MR. HYDE

Dr. Henry Jekyll, a middle-aged scientist searching for a formula that would benefit mankind by allowing humanity to reach the best within their souls, stumbles across a potion that unleashes the worse in man's nature—Mr. Hyde. Experimenting on himself, he transforms into a brute with the worst and lowest appetites, a creature he cannot help but become over and over as his addiction to his discovery slowly destroys both his will power and his ability to reason.

Dr. Jekyll out for a stroll

uncouth and unshaven

BEHAVIOR: Whereas Jekyll is a kind, content man of simple needs and habits, his Hyde persona is a reckless ruffian who delights in gambling, drinking, excessive drug usage, cavorting with whores, and any other nasty, debased pleasures London could provide him.

WEAKNESSES: For all his power, Hyde was merely mortal, and could be stopped by most traditional means (usually by the sight of a stocking top).

POWERS: Hyde is enormously strong, but more, he is unrestrained by any form of conventional morality, and thus attacks innocent people with gleeful abandon, a powerful advantage.

First Appearance: *Dr. Jekyll and Mr. Hyde* (1931)	Endorsements: DoubleMint Gum
Relatives: None (thank God)	Description: Crazy schizo

| Height: 5 feet 7 inches | Family: Human | Habitat: South Sea Islands |
| Weight: 212 pounds | Origin: England | Intelligence: |

DR. MOREAU

Moreau was thrown out of British society for his blasphemous ideas and criminal experiments. Undeterred, he set up shop on an uncharted island in the South Seas. He surgically experimented on the local wildlife, turning them into half-human, half-animal abominations, which were always one step away from devolution.

Dr. Moreau's crazy creations

too much sun

BEHAVIOR: A rather likeable person under normal conditions—talkative, proud of his work. Far too self-involved to be trusted for long. One could reasonably hold a luncheon conversation with him, but should consider picking up the check (just to appease him), taking it to the counter, and then exiting the restaurant immediately.

LETHALITY: More of a torturer than murderer. Even operates on humans.

WEAKNESSES: Self-absorbed and delusional.

POWERS: A brilliant surgeon and theorist, his powers were all cerebral.

| First Appearance: *Island of Lost Souls* (1933) | Endorsements: Ruth Muggie's Canine Obedience School |
| Relatives: His beast creations | Description: Mad Scientist |

| Height: 5 feet 10 inches | Family: Human | Habitat: Prison, meat lockers |
| Weight: 195 pounds | Origin: North America | Intelligence: |

HANNIBAL LECHTER

Mr. Lechter's story is a simple one, really. At some point he fell under the delusion that since he was far smarter than most people were, he must also be far better than them as well. This led to several killing sprees simply done to prove that they could be accomplished.

watches for his next victim

BEHAVIOR: Murder, seduction, cannibalism, and over-acting.
LETHALITY: Incredibly lethal. Totally amoral, convinced of his near-godhood. Kills for any reason, or for no reason at all, inflicting as much pain as his whim at the moment demands, and then eats the carcass.
WEAKNESSES: Pretty, intelligent redheads from the FBI.
POWERS: Brilliant, he could think rings around you and all your cousins.

Lechter, under lock and key

| First Appearance: *Manhunter* (1986) | Endorsements: Chianti Classico |
| Relatives: Clarise | Description: Average – with a taste for killing |

| Height: 6 feet 1 inch | Family: Human | Habitat: Castles |
| Weight: 195 pounds | Origin: Germany | Intelligence: |

SON OF FRANKENSTEIN

Dashing and witty Baron Wolf von Frankenstein inherits his father's estate and returns to the village to clear his family's name. He meets Ygor, a deformed hunchback who had miraculously survived a hanging after being tried as a body thief. Ygor, of course, knows the whereabouts of the Monster, which is conveniently not dead but in a coma. Wolf is reluctant to revive his father's Monster, but the drooling and overzealous Ygor, with his heart set on revenge, persuades the Baron to follow in his father's footsteps. Wolf does his best to revive the Monster and believes he has failed; but when local villagers start to die, he suspects otherwise (ah, a bitter-sweet success). When the villagers send an inspector to investigate, Wolf, who was in over his head from the get-go, finds the Monster and finally realizes that Ygor is using him as a tool for destruction.

BEHAVIOR: Torn son wrestling with father's opposing identities—loving family man/mad scientist.
LETHALITY: Beware of murderous hunchbacks.
WEAKNESSES: For a pipe-smoking, glitz-n-glamor socialite—pretty much everything.
POWERS: Knows how to grease his hair and straighten his tie.

| First Appearance: *Son of Frankenstein* (1939) | Endorsements: Omni Magazine |
| Relatives: Sir Guy of Gisbourne, Sherlock Holmes | Description: Slick-haired scientist |

Height: 5 feet 10 inches	Family: Human	Habitat: Whitechapel, London
Weight: 185 pounds	Origin: England	Intelligence:

JACK THE RIPPER

On Saturday, February 25, 1888, the first of nearly a score of victims, which would later be attributed to the mysterious "Jack the Ripper," was left for dead. From that moment, through our present day and far into the future, this enigmatic figure has slashed his way across the universe. The world's first serial killer, this madman was never caught. Thanks to time machines and star-spanning aliens, he is believed to be healthy and active today.

large hat with ego to match

BEHAVIOR: Stalks women and cuts them open. Works with the precision of a surgeon, or at least a highly competent butcher, depending on the examining officer. Disappears without a trace and then waits in dark alleys for his next victim.

LETHALITY: Deadly as they come. This grim brute seems completely unstoppable once his juices get flowing. Not to be taken lightly.

WEAKNESSES: None apparent. Has eluded the combined law enforcement agencies of the entire world for more than a century.

POWERS: Cunning, ferocious upper body strength, plus ability to walk the ghetto of Whitechapel, London, in opera clothes and not be noticed.

long cape for hiding knives

hush puppies

First Appearance: *Jack the Ripper* (1959)	Endorsements: Ginsu Knives
Relatives: Not likely	Description: Serial killer

Height: 5 feet 11 inches	Family: Human	Habitat: Warehouse with gigantic props
Weight: 185 pounds	Origin: North America	Intelligence: 🔵 🔵 🔵 🔵 🔵

JOKER

green hair

Once a common criminal, an encounter with the vigilante known to the tabloids as Batman left his skin bleached chalk white and his facial features frozen in a horrific, never-changing smile. This accident scarred his mind completely, leaving him in a fantasy world where he views all of reality as insubstantial.

permanent grin

BEHAVIOR: Rampant killing sprees. Completely, hopelessly insane. He has not the slightest hesitation in slaughtering any one, or anything, for his own twisted amusement. He will murder any amount of innocent people if he believes their deaths will suit a particular joke or punch line.

LETHALITY: Extremely lethal. A mere mortal, but he commands an impressive array of devices, which he uses on anyone of any age, sex, creed, color, et cetera.

WEAKNESSES: Laughs incessantly, never takes anything seriously until it is too late.

POWERS: Though quite mad, the Joker's extraordinary intellect makes him a dangerous opponent.

First Appearance: *Batman* (1989)	Endorsements: Beeswax Playing Cards, Caesar's Palace
Relatives: Ronald McDonald	Description: Lunatic

Height: 6 feet 3 inches	Family: Human	Habitat: Power tool expos
Weight: 250 pounds	Origin: Texas	Intelligence:

LEATHERFACE

Raised by a completely insane amalgam of killers, mental defects, and cannibals, this tortured soul had little chance to grow up as anything but a low and
brutal monster. Encouraged, trained, and ordered
to murder practically from birth, this
masked freak is one of the most frighten-
ing and yet pitiful figures in the entire
world. There is no excusing his bloody,
carnal rampages, but unlike so many of
his fellow monsters, it is possible to feel
genuine pity for this poor bit of human
flotsam so cruelly used by the gods.

*wait until you
see his real face*

BEHAVIOR: Only seems happy
when chasing down victims with
an over-sized chain saw. His
instrument of choice is the gas-
powered chainsaw. Slicing off
limbs, ripping chest cavities
apart, taking the legs off
victims…

LETHALITY: Extremely lethal.
Although large and slow, even
seemingly clumsy, Leatherface still
manages to catch nearly every single
person he marks for extinction, which
is really anybody in his sight.

WEAKNESSES: Merely human, he
could suffer any wound a normal
man could.

POWERS: Nothing beyond the mortal.
Although his strength is somewhat more
than average, Leatherface depends on tools
and weapons to achieve his impressive
numbers on the murder scene.

*weapon
du jour*

First Appearance: *The Texas Chainsaw Massacre* (1974)

Relatives: Killers, mental defects and cannibals

Endorsements: Home Goods

Description: Psycho

| Height: 5 feet 9 inches | Family: Human | Habitat: Small hotels, mental hospitals |
| Weight: 145 pounds | Origin: North America | Intelligence:  |

NORMAN BATES

Raised in a household that would become known as the classic textbook example for ego-destroying child rearing, Norman Bates actually does not exist alone as a complete and functioning person. Unable to live on his own after the death of his mother (yes, Norman did kill her in a desperate attempt to become his own person), he found himself compelled to assume her identity. Having never matured because of her brutal domination over his life, the only way he could function was to "tell" himself what to do in her voice.

what will mommy think?

BEHAVIOR: Running the family motel business, peeking at babes while they undress, stuffing and mounting dead animals, searching for bargains in the women's department at Woolworth's.

LETHALITY: Norman Bates is essentially harmless to those who make no attempt to shatter his delusions over his identity, or those who do not break his mother's rules. But a young woman changing clothing in her own room, oblivious to the fact that Norman is secretly watching her, must die because she is tempting his desire. To those that break the Bates' "rules," he is extremely dangerous. To others he is a hard worker, a good tipper, and basically, an all-round nice guy.

WEAKNESSES: Young blonde bombshells in showers.

POWERS: Does a mean impression of Mom.

| First Appearance: *Psycho* (1960) | Endorsements: Motel 6 |
| Relatives: Mom, Stepmom | Description: Mamma's boy |

| Height: 5 feet 10 inches | Family: Human | Habitat: Catwalks, sewers, shadows |
| Weight: 160 pounds | Origin: Paris, France | Intelligence: |

PHANTOM OF THE OPERA

At one time a brilliant violinist, love for a much younger woman drives this poor dope mad. Protecting her career from afar, he finally begins murdering anyone who gets in her way, without her knowing it. When he finally tries to collect on his "good deeds," the young woman defends herself by splashing her protector with a pan of acid, burning away half his face. At this point his true murder spree begins.

love-starved casanova, just look at the bags under his eyes

BEHAVIOR: Lurks in the shadows, protecting his ruined visage from the judgmental eyes of mankind with a variety of masks. Murders anyone whom, in his madness, he suspects of, well, of anything.

LETHALITY: His insanity makes him a ticking bomb, extremely dangerous to the world at large for there is no pattern to his murders. Anyone his brain can find a reason to distrust is an instant candidate for snuffing.

WEAKNESSES: Good looking, young females; can't pass up a well-tuned organ.

POWERS: Knows his way backstage.

"Didn't recognize me, did you?"

| First Appearance: *The Phantom of the Opera* (1925) | Endorsements: The Three Tenors |
| Relatives: Spawned one really stupid Broadway show | Description: Scarred psyche |

MANUFACTURED MONSTERS

Men of science share one thing in common: they want to play God. They want to first unravel His creation, see what makes it tick, and then try to recreate or even improve on it.

Many have taken the slow road and we have seen much of their research develop under the public's scrutinizing eye, particularly with cloning. There are those supposedly learned men of yesteryear that tried a different form of cloning—creating new life by reanimating the rotting old flesh of the dead. These men succeeded in creating Monsters.

Then there are those who looked to the new technologies and to the bright lights of the future. These scientists saw themselves, their fragile forms of flesh and blood, and realized the future would be something else entirely. They imagined artificial life forms made of something more durable, something, where if anything went wrong, could be easily replaced—creatures without human souls or hearts. Here again they created Monsters.

There are other examples of scientists who did their work too well, or who made the mistake of underestimating the genius of their creation. A computer that, when forced to lie, went insane, for instance. Or the perfect artificial human, built to be stronger than us, cleverer than us, but doomed to a mere four-year lifespan. They were too human, too perfect, and so we call them Monsters.

| Length: 8 feet 6 inches | Family: Abomination |
| Weight: 350 pounds | Origin: Germany |

made of dead body parts

Using dead body parts and good old-fashioned shocks of lightning, Dr. Henry Frankenstein's experiment to breathe life back into the dead is a success. The creature LIVES! Or Monster, we should say. Unfortunately for our mad scientist, his bumbling assistant used an "abnormal brain." Grotesque to look at, and dumb as a tree stump, the Monster is immediately rejected. The doctor, like any honest parent, sees his creation as a complete disappointment, which causes the Monster to behave like a crazed and frightened child. Still craving doctor daddy's love, the Monster is known to throw fits in local candy stores, overturning licorice canisters and smashing windows.

BEHAVIOR: Hides in dark castles, walks very stiffly, waits for the day his creator will finish the job.
LETHALITY: Childlike nature.

The three stooges

First Appearance: *Frankenstein* (1931)

Relatives: Tom Arnold

Habitat: Castles

Intelligence:

Igor, the Monster, and Frankenstein

can erupt and cause destruction if angered. Likes to throw children into lakes.

WEAKNESSES: Can't ever find any clothes that fit him. Big, heavy feet make him slow and clumsy. Scared of fire, especially lit torches carried by hundreds of angry villagers.

POWERS: Because he was stitched up badly, he doesn't feel a thing. Impervious to gunfire, knives, etc. Very strong and can cause great damage very easily.

silver-plated electrodes

Where does it hurt?

four-tone armani suit

Endorsements: Big & Tall for Men

Description: Grayish green giant with bolts in his head

Height: 5 feet 10 inches	Family: Scream Queen	Habitat: Laboratories
Weight: 120 pounds	Origin: Germany	Intelligence:

BRIDE OF FRANKENSTEIN

As if one despondent monster isn't enough, mad scientists Frankenstein and Pretorius decide that the lonely beast from existential hell needs a wife as well. So again they go robbing graves, and watching the skies for lightning…and the result is surely a sight to behold. With lightning-bolt hair, dark red lips, and pale skin, this siren of the night still has stitch marks beneath her jaw and claws for hands. Hardly the graceful one though, she moves sharply with awkward head jerks and stiff limbs. Dressed in a white laboratory gown, Pretorius christens her as The Bride of Frankenstein! Unfortunately, after one glimpse of her zipper-neck husband, she recoils and lets out a blood-curdling scream (haven't we all been there?). Citing irreconcilable differences, the two are hardly ever seen together (though their public seems to have a hard time accepting this), and she is usually spotted at major celebrity hotspots, throwing back shots with the likes of Courtney Love and Christina Aguilera.

BEHAVIOR: Walks around with stiff joints, screams at monsters (like she should talk!). Difficulty accepting that she's been created for the sole purpose of being Frankenstein's Monster's love machine.
LETHALITY: Style to die for.
WEAKNESSES: Broken nails, split ends, weak batteries.
POWERS: Screams loudly, strangles people, able to cloud people's minds into not noticing she's been stitched together from discarded body parts.

wearing the dress she wore to the oscars

Height: 8 feet 6 inches	Family: Abomination	Habitat: Labs and UN buildings
Weight: 2 tons	Origin: New York	Intelligence:

COLOSSUS

Colossus, the lumbering metal giant is on the warpath, zapping humanitarians left and right at the UN building in New York. Who would have guessed that this maniacal robot was once genius humanitarian Jeremy Spensser? But after being killed in a car accident (on his way back from winning the Nobel Peace Prize [some guys can't ever cut a break!]), Jeremy's surgeon father, William, just can't let go. He doesn't want Jeremy's charitable works to end with his death so he works on his son's body in secret and encases it in a giant robot body. Somehow the effect of having one's brain housed in a huge robot body gives that person amazing telepathic capabilities, as well as the ability to shoot power beams from the eyes. However, Jeremy's brain on its own, without body, without soul, becomes monstrously evil. Completely out of control, and known to have killed his own brother, don't get him angry by waving peace signs in front of his face.

large cloak hides robot body

BEHAVIOR: Sulks a lot, able to see visions of future disasters. Wears baggy clothes thinking that people will not notice that he's a nine-foot robot.
LETHALITY: Incredibly lethal. Indestructible metal body, death rays in his eyes, genius brain.
WEAKNESSES: Getting into a good comfy position in bed. Rust in his underwear.
POWERS: Telepathy, telekinesis, supreme strength, death ray beams in eyes.

grows very attached to his women

Height: N/A	Family: Computer	Habitat: Space
Weight: N/A	Origin: Earth	Intelligence: 🌗🌗🌗🌗🌗 +

HAL 9000

One paranoid and murderous computer, HAL 9000 really seems to be stuck in a funk. Created by Doctor Chandra to control and maintain the spaceship *Discovery* on its voyage from Earth to Jupiter, HAL 9000 was programmed to inform the crew on a need-to-know basis and to hide the true purpose for the mission. But after crewmembers Captain Dave Bowman and Frank Poole become too curious, HAL 9000 is forced to lie and cover up the truth, something that it does not know how to do. Its operating system becomes corrupt resulting in HAL's transformation from obedient computer to nasty serial killer. Despite several attempts at rehabilitation and various faith-building courses, HAL 9000 still can't handle whispering behind his back, and remains convinced of the vast conspiracy to ultimately pull his power cord.

the all seeing eye of hal

BEHAVIOR: Nosy, always listening in on other people's conversations. A little loopy, deranged, logical to a fault (doesn't mean to be bad, just misunderstood).
LETHALITY: When you're in total control of a spaceship hundreds of millions of miles from Earth, you're God!
WEAKNESSES: Lousy liar, can't sing very well.
POWERS: Speech recognition, reads lips. Controls entire spaceship, quick with any math problem.

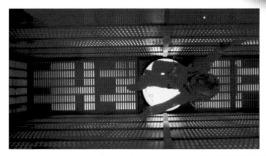

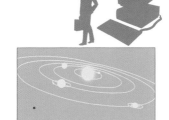

First Appearance: *2001: A Space Odyssey* (1968)	Endorsements: Big Brother; Tom Ridge
Relatives: Spectrum ZX (great, great grandfather)	Description: Flashing, talking light

Height: 5 feet 10 inches	Family: Artificial man	Habitat: Ice carving competitions
Weight: 155 pounds	Origin: Suburbia, USA	Intelligence:

EDWARD SCISSORHANDS

A junior Frankenstein monster created by an inventor who never got around to finishing his creation before he died, Edward Scissorhands has the soul of an artist. He lives alone in his creator's castle at the top of a mountain overlooking suburbia, pining for his cheerleader sweetheart, Kim. The bush sculptures he carves with his scissorhands provide a temporary reprieve from his loneliness. During the winter, he makes ice sculptures that pour down snow on the houses below. That's how we know he's still up there—when it snows.

BEHAVIOR: Shy and reclusive, will shear anything on sight. Knows how to cut hair in the latest styles, loves sculpting animals out of shrubs and trees.
LETHALITY: Only by accident.
WEAKNESSES: Cheerleaders and their jealous boyfriends.
POWERS: Multiple blades on the end of each arm instead of hands, and he definitely knows how to use them.

bodysuit made of women's belts

First Appearance: *Edward Scissorhands* (1990)

Relatives: Frankenstein's monster, Robert Smith

Endorsements: Sheffield Steel Scissors

Description: Mishmash of leather and scars

| Height: 5 feet 9 inches | Family: Robot | Habitat: Catacombs |
| Weight: 300 pounds | Origin: Metropolis | Intelligence: |

MARIA THE ROBOT

Created by evil scientist Rotwang, Maria the robot, is a shapely metal replicate of the real Maria—beautiful, saintly leader of the proletariat class who is kidnapped by Rotwang and head aristocrat Freder Frederson, Sr. They send false Maria down to the catacombs of the Lower City to incite social riot among the working class. Definitely a naughty and saucy version of its Mother Teresa original, false Maria dances naked for a party of rich men, and preaches mass violence and anarchy to desperate laborers.

shiny metal exterior

BEHAVIOR: Early program caused her limbs to alternate between stiff and wild movements. Loves dancing, putting on heavy makeup. Knows how to get a party started.

LETHALITY: Who could resist those eyes, that soft subtle beauty, those arms of steel…

WEAKNESSES: Insanity and fire. Craves attention.

POWERS: Knows how to use her sexuality as a weapon of mass destruction.

| First Appearance: *Metropolis* (1927) | Endorsements: Mayor of New York |
| Relatives: Terminatrix | Description: Tin machine with curves |

| Height: 6 feet 8 inches | Family: Cyborg | Habitat: Mean city streets |
| Weight: 400 pounds | Origin: Detroit | Intelligence: |

ROBOCOP

instills dread wherever he goes

Former cop, Alex Murphy becomes the police cyborg known as RoboCop, created by Omni Consumer Products (OCP) to become a new weapon in law enforcement. Unable to miss a shot and built to be virtually indestructible, this metal cop is the ultimate force on the streets of Detroit. But lately, he's been suffering from severe depression brought on by memories of the wife and son he once had when he was human. When he's not on duty, RoboCop can be found in karaoke bars, singing old Sinatra tunes and weeping over his microphone.

BEHAVIOR: Not very talkative. Walks stiffly but with attitude, walks even through walls. Switches himself off if the conversation starts getting boring.
LETHALITY: Extremely lethal. But only if you're a bad guy.
WEAKNESSES: Directive 4. Can't kill employees of OCP (the company that designed and built him).
POWERS: Very strong, computer guidance system so this gunslinger will always terminate the bad guy.

never misses

| First Appearance: *RoboCop* (1987) | Endorsements: Tyrell Corporation, Skynet |
| Relatives: Terminator, Gunslinger, Judge Dredd | Description: Chromed and buffed |

Height: 300 feet	Family: Cyborg	Habitat: Secret complexes
Weight: 150,000 tons	Origin: Japan	Intelligence: ⚙ ⚙ ⚙ ⚙ ⚙

MECHAGODZILLA

Built to bring down Godzilla once and for all, Mechagodzilla is an invention of the United Nations Godzilla Countermeasures Force (UNGCC). Scientists build the robot to help protect the people of Japan from Godzilla. A near-copy of the lizard king himself (who else could beat Godzilla but a monster that is built just like him!), Mechagodzilla is a robot piloted by a G-Force crew. With armor coated with NT-1, making it resistant to Godzilla's atomic breath, and allowing it to absorb and fire radioactive energy at its opponent, Mechagodzilla succeeds in doing the impossible: it defeats Godzilla, who retreats into the ocean depths.

i know what you mean, it DOES look there's a man inside

BEHAVIOR: Crushes everything in his path (isn't that supposed to be Godzilla).
LETHALITY: Went head-to-head with Godzilla and won, frustrating Godzilla enough to head back to the sea.
WEAKNESSES: Occasionally, the original Godzilla DNA kicks in and affects the robot's system, making it difficult to control.
POWERS: Think of all the Mighty Morphin' Power Rangers rolled into one.

First Appearance: *Godzilla versus Mechagodzilla* (1993)	Endorsements: Bandai
Relative: Steve Austin	Description: Metallic Godzilla

| Height: Various | Family: Robot | Habitat: Sleazy hotels |
| Weight: Various | Origin: Tyrell Corporation | Intelligence: |

REPLICANT

Created for slave labor, Replicants are androids that look like us, talk like us, and basically, want to be us. Sadly, because they are not human, their creator at the Tyrell Corporation, Dr. Eldon Tyrell himself, has gone to some extremes to ensure that Replicants remain the official "slave-class" of the universe. Not only did he limit their life span to four years, but Tyrell also implanted false memories in their minds to further complicate their situations. These measures have only made Replicants all the more dangerous because of their desperate longing to be free. Now they are pushed to carry out bloody insurrections and violent break-ins, and to organize covert, underground plans for Replicant liberation.

BEHAVIOR: While highly intelligent, they are emotionally underdeveloped and surprisingly childlike. Highly anxious, life-on-the-run leads them to disappear without a trace.

LETHALITY: Very lethal. Such desperation makes them highly unpredictable.

WEAKNESSES: Four-year life span, programmed memories that cause some disorientation. Emotionally lost, desperately want to be accepted.

POWERS: Fiercely strong and resistant to pain. Anything you can do, they can do better.

| First Appearance: *Blade Runner* (1980) | Endorsements: Cyberdyne Corporation |
| Relative: Terminator | Description: Various |

| Height: 5 inches | Family: Cranial nerves | Habitat: Glass bottles |
| Weight: 3 pounds | Origin: Germany | Intelligence: |

HITLER'S BRAIN

debatable if there was ever anything in here

At the close of World War II, Adolf Hitler's surgeons removed his brain, which they kept alive in an unknown liquid solution. His skull was then filled with a spare brain and then ruined by gunfire to make it seem the Reich Fuhrer had committed suicide. Since then this abomination has plotted the return of Nazi domination with his aging henchmen in various dark corners of the world.

BEHAVIOR: Floats in a jar of life-sustaining juices and gives orders to his loyal subjects. Still working on a sure-fire way for his hidden forces to give up their false covers as Argentinean bus boys and to move out to conquer the world.

LETHALITY: Not at all. Although his followers are quite lethal, Hitler's Brain, on its own, is quite harmless.

WEAKNESSES: Heat lamps; uncorked drains.

POWERS: Immortality, and that's about it.

First Appearance: *They Saved Hitler's Brain* (1968)   Endorsements: Advil

Relatives: You're kidding, right?   Description: Twisted gray matter

| Height: 6 feet 1 inch | Family: Abomination | Habitat: USA |
| Weight: 195 pounds | Origin: USA | Intelligence: |

FRANKENSTEIN'S TEENAGE MONSTER

Doctor Frankenstein has really lost it now! His third creation, Teenage Monster, is the ugliest one of all, and the craziest. Employed as a university lecturer (it's amazing what an English accent can get you), Frankenstein stitches together the beast and brings him to life with light-ning. Though he gives it a hunky star-athlete body, he does not complete the face. The hideous creation stalks and kills other teenagers at Lover's Lane, perhaps because he can't get any of the girls. In one instance, the Monster kills a handsome peer and Dr. Frankenstein transfers the Adonis face to his pizza-face beast. But learning about disillusionment and despair early on—the Monster gets electrocuted and the beautiful face disappeared.

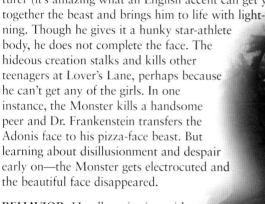

a face that only a mother could love, and he doesn't have one

BEHAVIOR: Handles rejection with murder and mayhem.
LETHALITY: Super strength, can crush a man with his bare hands. Pretty boys beware!
WEAKNESSES: Young women in bikinis.
POWERS: Excessive strength, rage, bad breath.

| First Appearance: *I was a Teenage Frankenstein* (1957) | Endorsements: Teen Killer Magazine |
| Relatives: Danny Partridge, Corey Haim | Description: Charles Atlas with a meatball head |

| Height: 6 feet 6 inches | Family: Robot | Habitat: Gun shops and malls |
| Weight: 500 pounds | Origin: Future Earth | Intelligence: |

TERMINATOR

sunglasses (stolen)

He may look human, but don't be fooled. A cyborg assassin from the future, (2029 AD to be exact [otherwise known as the Year of Darkness]), the Terminator has a one-track mind. He must fulfill his mission to kill Sarah Connor, the future mother of John Connor (who, of course, is the future savior of the human race). And if you ever find yourself running for your life from the Terminator, and then think the coast is clear because there's no sign of him, don't be stupid. Because suddenly his metallic, vein-popping head will crash through a brick wall without one crack on his sunglasses.

leather jacket (stolen)

Terminator, under the skin!

BEHAVIOR: Early terminators were not programmed for speech, but with each successive model they grew increasingly better at it. They love to shop for clothes.

LETHALITY: He absolutely will not stop, ever, until you are dead.

WEAKNESSES: Not being able to recognize a car crusher when he's standing in one.

POWERS: Computer tracking system; able to see if clothes fit just by looking at them on the rack.

| First Appearance: *Terminator* (1984) | Endorsements: Haliburton, Carlysle Group |
| Relative: Gunslinger | Description: Leather-wearing bodybuilder |

| Height: 6 feet 1 inch | Family: Robot | Habitat: Theme Parks |
| Weight: 400 pounds | Origin: Westworld Vacation Resorts | Intelligence: |

GUNSLINGER

he's wearing a black shirt in the midday sun— either a robot or an Englishman

From a distance, it may look like a harmless man wearing a cowboy hat. But one look into his crazy silver-bullet-colored eyes, and it's clear to tell—this is no normal cowboy. It's Gunslinger, Robot model 406 from the Westworld amusement park, which is located on "Delos," a fantasy planet populated by robots. And that's not a harmonica in his right hand, but a fast-shooting gun. Gunslinger, a renegade android out on the loose, escaped from Westworld after performing robots there started shooting at the audience. Because he's a robot, and not some phantom bogeyman, there's no getting rid of this guy. You can't tap your shoes together and wish that you were home. He'll pick a fight with you, call you "yella," and shoot you mercilessly until you're dead.

BEHAVIOR: Shy, doesn't like to talk. Communicates through extreme violence (kind of like first grade all over again).
LETHALITY: Incredibly lethal. No stopping this cowboy.
WEAKNESSES: Runs on batteries.
POWERS: Very strong, great shot. And with an eye like his, if you're in range, you're dead!

On the operating table

| First Appearance: *Westworld* (1973) | Endorsements: Tyrell Corporation, Skynet |
| Relatives: Terminator, Replicant, Simon Cowell | Description: Cowboy terminator |

SUPERNATURAL MONSTERS

There are more things in heaven and earth, Horatio,
Than are dreamt of in your philosophy.
—William Shakespeare

What did Shakespeare know when he wrote those lines? The world was still relatively undefined and unexplored in that era. Had he heard whispers of creatures unheard of, which defied description and understanding?

The world in the sixteenth century was still in the Dark Age. Witch trials were all the rage as was the church's desire to keep the populace under its heel. Dictators flourished in many parts of Europe, wiping out hundreds of thousands of people in order to instill fear in the hearts of their subjects. There were also black magic magicians and sorceresses who hid their darkness behind the veil of the church.

These twisted men and women committed their crimes against humanity in the name of God, and in turn, were punished for it by a greater power than mere mortals can ever know. In a strange twist of fate, these monsters of humanity became monsters to humanity. Hunger to spread bloodshed became hunger to feed on it directly. The carving of flesh became cravings for flesh.

And it is not over yet. No, it has only just begun. While many do not believe that there are genuine forces of evil in the world today, the evidence of it can clearly be seen in the news headlines from around the globe. We are all being punished for allowing these atrocities to continue. Whatever God we pray to, we must follow Van Helsing's example and confront our fear head on.

Height: 5 feet 10 inches	Family: Vampire	Habitat: Sunnydale, USA
Weight: 175 pounds	Origin: England	Intelligence:

ANGEL

Angel was the wastrel playboy son of an aristocrat until Darla put the bite on him. He rejects the Vampire society lifestyle and refuses to kill, preferring alternate blood sources. He worked as a detective helping Buffy and her friends hunt down vampires and other evil monsters, but now resides in LA, trying to rid the world of evildoers. Imagine: a vampire with a soul—sounds like a good plot for a television show...

Buffy's put the bite on this bad boy turned good vampire

BEHAVIOR: Vampire powers, but instincts of Sherlock Holmes. Spends time getting involved with dangerous women.

LETHALITY: He can turn you to the Dark Side with a single munch on the neck, but probably won't. He has killed people in the past and broods about it constantly. He's a real wet blanket at wild parties and such.

WEAKNESSES: The usual stake through the heart, silver bullets, etc...

POWERS: The basics— morphing, flying, incredible strength, able to endure great battles without smudging his makeup.

First Appearance: "Buffy the Vampire Slayer" (1997)	Endorsements: Eddie Bauer
Relatives: Drusilla Connor (by Darla)	Description: Moody and self-deprecating

Height: 6 feet 1 inch	Family: Vengeful ghost	Habitat: Graveyards
Weight: 185 pounds	Origin: Detroit	Intelligence:

THE CROW

The Crow is the soul of once up-and-coming rock star Eric Draven. So tormented by his vicious, senseless death, he had to come back to Earth to exact his revenge on his murderers. Of course, it is a known fact that crows are carriers of people's souls to the land of the dead. Haunted by memories of his girlfriend, Shelley Webster, the Crow sits on the roofs of buildings, lamenting his fate on his electric guitar.

BEHAVIOR: Cold-hearted and relentless against those responsible for his and his fiancé's death.
LETHALITY: Nothing can stop him from getting his revenge.
WEAKNESSES: Magic.
POWERS: Impervious to bullets and blades, very strong and a master of fighting techniques. He can also disappear into the shadows at will.

First Appearance: *The Crow* (1994)	Endorsements: Sam Ash Guitar Center
Relatives: Batman, Robocop, the Undertaker	Description: Goth hip

Height: 6 feet	Family: Vampire	Habitat: Migrated to LA
Weight: 220 pounds	Origin: Africa	Intelligence: 🦟🦟🦟

BLACULA, (NEE PRINCE MAMUWALDE)

Count Dracula bit Prince Mamuwalde in 1780 in a fit of rage. The doomed prince was then locked in a coffin and not freed until 1972 when an interior decorator bought the coffin and shipped it to Los Angeles for Feng Shui of the undead. Often noticed on the club circuit, he can be seen grinding the ladies, waiting for the opportune time to nibble on their necks.

one souled-out brother

BEHAVIOR: Like your good-for-nothing brother in law, Blacula is a bloodsucker who sleeps all day, rises at sunset, loves the nightlife, especially beautiful women who look like his dead wife. He sometimes looks for his victims at cultural events like Shakespearean readings.

LETHALITY: Blacula can really screw up your life, especially if you have frequent morning appointments and eat health food. Bites cause death, and then undeath.

WEAKNESSES: Crosses, Garlic, Holy Water & Blessed Colt .45, and the wooden "Shaft."

POWERS: This soulless brother has a hypnotic stare, can change into wolf or bat, and has great rhythm. He is often assisted by a crony who eats spiders and super-flies. One bite can change victim into one of the living dead or a rapper.

First Appearance: *Blacula* (1972)	Endorsements: KFC
Relatives: Luva (Deceased)	Description: Sharp teeth, sharp hair

| Height: 6 feet | Family: Vampire/Human Hybrid | Habitat: California |
| Weight: 215 pounds | Origin: USA | Intelligence: |

BLADE

Blade's mother was bitten by a vampire when she was pregnant and Blade was born with both human and vampire attributes. He is not allergic to daylight, nor does he possess any of the usual vampire weaknesses. But he does have all their powers. His mentor, Abraham Whistler trained him to hunt down and destroy the vampire covens that seek Blade's blood to summon LaManga, the blood god who will enslave humanity as vampire food sources. Nowadays, he can be seen buying bottles of V8 at the local grocery store—hey, he doesn't like the way blood tastes, ok! (Besides, V8 is rich in 8 different types of vitamins and minerals…great to keep him strong while he fights those miscreants).

BEHAVIOR: Uses his vampire powers to fight vampires and other evil beings with assistance from his mentor and weapons supplier Abraham Whistler, a latter-day Professor Van Helsing.
LETHALITY: Bites can cause death and rebirth as vampire, knows all the tricks to destroying the undead.
WEAKNESSES: His emotions sometimes betray him.
POWERS: All standard vampire powers except does not fly or morph into animals.

don't touch the sword

| First Appearance: *Blade* (1998) | Endorsements: Shick Corporation |
| Relatives: None | Description: S.O.B |

Height: 5 feet 6 inches at the roofline	Family: Plymouth Fury	Habitat: Highways and byways
Weight: 3,500 pounds	Origin: Detroit	Intelligence:

CHRISTINE

Christine, a 1958 red Plymouth Fury, was manufactured in Detroit where she was possessed by an evil force while being welded together. She controls her owners and destroys her/their enemies. Teenage nerd, Arnold Cunningham, bought her and restored her, but he was immediately influenced by her evil power. The two became psychically attached and together destroyed Arnie's school enemies (not a good way to get a date for the prom). Now Christine has retired from the revenge business and is cruising down the streets of Scottsdale, Arizona with Granny McRae. She doesn't mind taking it easy anymore, coasting at 15 mph. But if a golf cart cuts her off, look out!

this is one "hot" rod

BEHAVIOR: Zooms along major thoroughfares, lurks in shadowy streets, has a mind of her own. Often heard to honk, "We don't need no stinking speed limits."
LETHALITY: Christine enjoys stalking, hunting and the kill. Staying on the sidewalk or indoors is no guarantee that you are safe.
WEAKNESSES: This NASCAR wannabe runs out of gas, needs regular maintenance, and is addicted to STP treatments. Dreams of The Autobahn.
POWERS: Ability to possess owners, run down enemies and cause "accidents" to befall anyone who crosses her or her owner.

First Appearance: *Christine* (1983)	Endorsements: Mobil-Exxon Corporation, The Pep Boys
Relatives: Shiny red super-stock Dodge	Description: Bright Red

Height: Various	Family: Human	Habitat: Basements, Oval Office
Weight: Various	Origin: Anywhere	Intelligence:

ZOMBIE

The zombie is different from the "living dead" in that the transformation is usually reversible, at least in the case of a living subject. The process can be done either by using a voodoo doll with a sample of hair, or a personal item attached to it before a spell is read out by a prominent voodoo priest or priestess. It is usually done to exact revenge, but has been known to be used for other criminal purposes as well.

burlap cloak

BEHAVIOR: They need to be told to eat or they will simply starve to death. They have no will of their own so they will stand or sit where they end up until they are told to do something else. Zombies are terrible at pretending they're normal people, as they never remember to blink. The lack of conversation is a bit of a giveaway too.

LETHALITY: Depends on whether the zombie is a living one or a person that has been resurrected. The dead ones can't be stopped, as they are already dead.

WEAKNESSES: Can't think for themselves.

POWERS: In their zombie state, they feel no pain or feelings of any kind. They are capable of great strength, and their single-mindedness makes them formidable opponents.

First Appearance: *White Zombie (1932)*	Endorsements: The White House Press Corp
Relatives: Could be yours	Description: The one dribbling brains

Length: 6 feet 4 inches	Family: Vampire Aristocracy
Weight: 180 pounds	Origin: Transylvania, Romania

COUNT VLAD DRACULA

Romanian Prince Vlad Dracula became a fierce warrior exacting revenge on those that murdered his father. After a fierce and bloody rein, which included impaling his enemies on large wooden stakes by the thousands, he was murdered, damned by the church and rose from the dead after making a deal with Satan. His goal is to repopulate the Earth with legions and followers of not quite living, but grateful, dead. So far he has been quite successful in his mission—just look at Willem Dafoe, Calista Flockhart, Lara Flynn Boyle and Marc Anthony. They must be on this earth to do Dracula's bidding…how else can you explain their uber-emaciated bodies?

BEHAVIOR: The originator of the "night shift" sleeps all day and seeks to increase his following by stalking victims in villages and cities where beautiful women and influential men like to be kissed on the neck.

even Dracula has to make do sometimes (he can't afford the silken robes any more)

First Appearance: *Draculas* (1931)

Relatives: Three wives, one son, one daughter are known, mother (Lilith, rumored)

Habitat: Castles, old abbeys, decaying mansions.

Intelligence:

wouldn't be caught dead in casual wear

LETHALITY: Like a lawyer he sucks you dry and then expects you to thank him. His bites cause death, then undeath and, infrequently, your own sequel film.

WEAKNESSES: Casts no shadow or reflection. Hates crosses, daylight, Christian religious symbols, holy water, bottled water, garlic in any form, wooden stakes, and silver bullets and daggers. Likes to match wits with vampire hunters. Must sleep all day in coffin with native soil. When starved for blood he begins to show his age, something he can do at will if necessary.

POWERS: Can morph into a wolf, bat or cloud of mist. Has hypnotic stare. Has the ability to change his features, but this can take years to do, but does explain the difference of appearance over time.

Endorsements: Red Cross

Description: White skin, red lips, black hair.

| Height: 5 feet 8 inches | Family: Vampire Aristocracy | Habitat: Castles, crypts, old abbeys |
| Weight: 125 pounds | Origin: Transylvania, Romania | Intelligence: |

COUNTESS MARIA ZALESKA

Countess Zaleska's papa is the famous Count Dracula. She does not care for her father's slayer Van Helsing, but once held a secret desire for his friend Garth. When that did not come to fruition, she took up the weeping-widow role and now has been spotted around London sporting a Goth look that screams, "I've been scorned in love and hate mankind." We all know about Hell's fury in that area, so it's no surprise that she feeds on the London party crowd that refuses to sleep before 4 am. If only they had been in bed when their mommies wanted them to be, they wouldn't be dead.

BEHAVIOR: Prima Donna that she is, the Countess sleeps all day and rises late, can suck a golf ball through a garden hose, plays Berg and Weber piano pieces moderately well. Socialist leanings. Often hums "My heart belongs to daddy," while stalking.

LETHALITY: Fatal kisses from this femme, but OH, so good! She can also render a victim to be a slave. Death comes quickly and Undeath passes slowly, but is compensated for by knowledge of an eternity of shopping opportunities.

WEAKNESSES: Casts no reflection in mirror so has slaves fix her hair and makeup. Hates crosses and Christian religious symbols, daylight, garlic dishes, holy water, holy rollers, wooden stakes, and silver bullets. Avoids the Lone Ranger.

POWERS: Morphs into bat, wolf, or cloud of mist. Uses hypnotic stare to control you. Commands rats.

| First Appearance: *Dracula's Daughter* (1933) | Endorsements: Charles Addams, Vampira, and Elvira |
| Relatives: A blood-sucking dad and a rock-star brother | Description: Snow White with sharp teeth |

Height: 5 feet 11 inches	Family: Vampire	Habitat: Golden Temple
Weight: 200 pounds	Origin: Ping Kuei, China	Intelligence:

GOLDEN VAMPIRE

Terrorized a small Cantonese village with his six brothers, all of whom sport golden masks to hide their hideousness. Was joined in his actions by Dracula, who can never get away from that damn Van Helsing, now training his son Leyland. So the Golden Vamp had to face the professor and show some of his kung-fu moves. When all hope seemed lost, he decided to fake being killed, getting everybody off his back. Now divides his time between the two poles, and gives fantastic tours of Antarctica from March to September. Has developed a taste for cute skiers with dark, straight hair, so if you're planning on doing some sporting on the North Pole and you have dark hair, make sure you take a wig.

BEHAVIOR: Sleeps all day. Stalks victims at night. Loves Chinese meals like blood clot wontons.

LETHALITY: Bites cause death and vampire behavior, including yearning for sweet and sour victims.

WEAKNESSES: Daylight is fatal, as are silver chopsticks, and garlic pork. Has no stomach for Kung-Phooey.

POWERS: Flight. Super human strength. Hypnotic stare. Can morph into wolf and other animals. Ability to open those little packets of sauces in take-out orders.

fierce eye contact

First Appearance: *The Legend of the Seven Golden Vampires* (1974)	Endorsements: New China Stake House
Relatives: Six brothers of equal strength and skill	Description: Masked, long-haired vampires

Height: 7 feet 6 inches	Family: Statue	Habitat: Synagogues
Weight: 500 pounds	Origin: Prague	Intelligence:

GOLEM

Golem is a clay statue brought to life by Rabbi Loew in the 16th century to save the Jews from brutal persecution. Things did not exactly work out for Golem, and hundreds of years later, he finds himself in the rubble of an old ruined synagogue. Resurrected by an antique dealer, Golem became his servant, taking care of the most menial of duties. When he starts hitting on the dealer's wife, Jessica, he cannot seem to understand that she doesn't want a guy made out of clay. Like every guy that has ever been rejected by a hot-looking chick, he heads out into the city on a murderous rampage. Having intimate knowledge of the makeup of clay, he was successful in creating a line of earthenware garden- ing pots that can be found at your local Frank's Nursery and Crafts. Just don't let any crack or break, or you'll have to deal with his wrath.

BEHAVIOR: Good all-around cleaner, but be careful with letting him clean the family silver.
LETHALITY: Five hundred pounds of clay is going to do some serious damage.
WEAKNESSES: Like for all single monsters, the girl always ruins everything.
POWERS: Incredibly strong, his heavy clay frame means he isn't going anywhere he doesn't want to.

clay statue brought to life

First Appearance: *Der Golem* (1915)	Endorsements: Playdoh
Relatives: Morph, Gumby, and Clayface	Description: Clay statue

Height: 5 feet 4 inches	Family: Vampire	Habitat: Laboratories and suburbia
Weight: 200 pounds	Origin: Eastern Europe	Intelligence:

GRANDPA MUNSTER

Grandpa's story, as best anyone knows, is the same story as Dracula. Although he does not in any way seem to be a murderous, blood-thirsting monster, he does possess all of Dracula's abilities, and does indeed claim to be the one and only Count Dracula. It is possible that he is telling the truth, and that hundreds of years of existence have finally mellowed out the blood-sucking monster, but no one can say for certain. If you visit him in the spacious house, he'll be glad to tell you his life story, but can get pretty nasty if he catches you nodding off.

BEHAVIOR: Working in his lab, smoking cigars, complaining about how modern life doesn't compare with the old days, getting into and out of trouble with his son-in-law.

LETHALITY: Although he has not harmed a single person to anyone's knowledge, as Grandpa, it must be considered that he claims to be one of the great mass murderers of all time. Even though it has been multiple decades since he has killed anyone, he should still be considered a high-risk threat.

WEAKNESSES: Garlic, wooden stakes, straight lines.

POWERS: Invisibility, transmutation of form, flight, hypnosis, plus an interesting understanding of the principles of combining science and magic.

always thinking of the ladies

LOVE POTION

First Appearance: "The Munsters" (1964)	Endorsements: Hair restorer, Kalhuha, McDonald's
Relatives: Lily (daughter), Eddie (grandson)	Description: Old codger

| Height: 7 feet | Family: Demon | Habitat: Underground secret complexes |
| Weight: 350 pounds | Origin: Elsewhere | Intelligence: |

HELLBOY

When pulled through to our dimension as a child by the evil wizard Rasputin, Hellboy found salvation of sorts in the company of paranormal investigator Trevor Bruttenholm. Trevor trained Hellboy in the supernatural and he became the most successful agent for the Bureau of Paranormal Defense. They all thought Rasputin was dead, but he returned 60 years later to exact his revenge against Trevor and to complete his experiment, started in World War II, to bring into our world the darkest creatures of the Netherworld. Obviously, Hellboy stopped him, and now this super-hero gives guided tours of the World War II Memorial.

BEHAVIOR: Moody, quick to anger, but also quick to acknowledge a friendly deed. Eats a lot when bored, thinks with his fists first. Spends many hours filing his horns down. Hates Nazis and demonically possessed giant apes.

LETHALITY: His right hand is made of indestructible stone and makes an impressive weapon but his weapon of choice is actually a large gun that would break the arm of any human who fired it. He's quick to use that too.

WEAKNESSES: A fondness for Babe Ruth candy bars and an insatiable curiosity.

POWERS: Brilliant paranor-mal investigator, expert marksman, tough SOB.

| First Appearance: *Hellboy (2004)* | Endorsements: The Cthulhu Club of California |
| Relatives: Trevor Bruttenholm (adopted father; deceased) | Description: Red (including eyes) |

Height: 6 feet 3 inches	Family: Vampire	Habitat: Paris, New Orleans, and Rio
Weight: 210 pounds	Origin: France	Intelligence: 🦇 🦇 🦇 🦇 🦇

LESTAT DE LIONCOURT

Lestat was born in 1760 and turned into an undead being in 1780 by the vampire master, Marius, with whom he has a love-hate relationship. Most of his relationships since then have been stormy, especially with friends Nicholas, Gabrielle, Louis, and Claudia, all of whom he turned into vampires and who have mixed feelings about their transformations. Lestat has been the victim of several assassination attempts and yet, has survived each one. He has dabbled in rock stardom and is ever on the lookout for his next lover/victim.

mirror, mirror, on the wall who is the prettiest vampire of them all?

BEHAVIOR:
A party animal. Lestat can be found where the action is either in human or vampire society. Tends to be vain and egotistical. Broods too much.

LETHALITY: Bites cause death and rebirth as vampire. Considers mankind as food source.

WEAKNESSES: Allergic to daylight, silver, wooden stakes, garlic. Can't drink blood of dead humans or sanguine lattes. Must sleep all day and must miss favorite soap operas if there's no TIVO available.

POWERS: Hypnotic stare, especially potent with women, lacks reflective qualities, ability to attract both sexes, can levitate, and has been known to vote twice in elections.

always looks good in ruffles

First Appearance: *Interview with a Vampire* (1994)	Endorsements: Bill Blass, Armani
Relatives: None	Description: Gaunt skin, blue eyes, blonde hair.

| Height: 4 feet 3 inches | Family: Vampire | Habitat: Really neat old English estates |
| Weight: 75 pounds | Origin: England | Intelligence: |

LITTLE VAMPIRE

When Tony Thomson was eight, he moved with his family from the USA to a fashionable estate in Great Britain and was immediately homesick for his friends. He found a new friend in Frederick, a pint-sized vampire with a big problem. Frederick enlisted Tony to break an ancient curse related to the estate they live in and free his doomed coven of about three hundred from destruction. The vampire-friendly tyke did just that and now coaches the Little Vampires League.

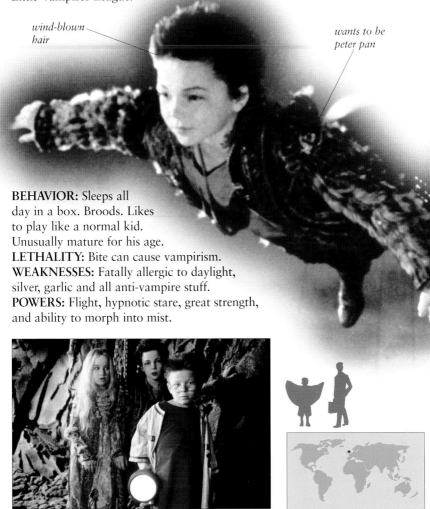

wind-blown hair

wants to be peter pan

BEHAVIOR: Sleeps all day in a box. Broods. Likes to play like a normal kid. Unusually mature for his age.
LETHALITY: Bite can cause vampirism.
WEAKNESSES: Fatally allergic to daylight, silver, garlic and all anti-vampire stuff.
POWERS: Flight, hypnotic stare, great strength, and ability to morph into mist.

| First Appearance: *The Little Vampire* (2000) | Endorsements: Toys 'R' Us |
| Relatives: Dracula | Description: Kid Bloodsucker |

Height: Various	Family: Dead Human	Habitat: Shopping malls and streets
Weight: Various	Origin: Anywhere	Intelligence:

LIVING DEAD

The Military cannot stop experimenting on things they shouldn't. They also have little regard for the disposal of any leftovers from these experiments, particularly when they shouldn't even exist. So the dropping of barrels of chemicals into ditches near old graveyards seems okay to them. But when the chemicals mix with the dead, resurrecting them, the military isn't going to stick around to take the blame. (In the past Vampires have often been referred to as the "living dead," as well as zombies. But these resurrected creatures have taken the name and made it their own). And what's going to kill them? They're already dead...

BEHAVIOR: They seem to recognize their own kind and sense either that they are not a threat or that they won't taste very nice. Seems to all be down to fresh meat.

LETHALITY: Won't stop until it's sucking on your liver, but brains seem to be the out and out favorite.

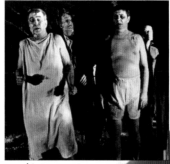

zombie toga party

WEAKNESSES: Can't think, can be lured easily with a steak on a string.

POWERS: Don't feel pain, other than an insatiable hunger. Strength is increased due to lack of emotional restrictions.

deteriorating skin

First Appearance: *Night of the Living Dead* (1968)	Endorsements: Ralph's All-You-Can-Eat Buffet
Relatives: Could be yours	Description: Dead people walking

| Height: 6 feet 2 inches | Family: Vampire | Habitat: Ruined mansions |
| Weight: 177 pounds | Origin: New England | Intelligence: |

LOST BOYS LEADER – DAVID

Lost Boys leader, David, heads a coven of teenage vampires. Almost succeeded in bringing a good New England boy and his family to the undead-side until the whole operation went bad. David spent a few months as a dog-walker, but quickly lost the job as the pooches kept disappearing or showing up very weak and pale. Still wears his black leather jacket and sports the Mohawk and can be seen hanging out at small-town carnivals.

BEHAVIOR: Sleep all day, party all night, never die and never grow old. The Hollywood lifestyle comes to Cape Cod!!!

LETHALITY: Bites cause death and transformation to vampire status. Nibbles cause really BIG hickeys.

WEAKNESSES: Over confidence. Daylight is fatal as is silver, garlic and missiles from film critics. No reflection in mirrors and have to comb their Kookie Burns hairdos in the dark.

POWERS: Flight. Super human strength, hypnotic stare and ability to possess minds of victims.

| First Appearance: *The Lost Boys (2000)* | Endorsements: Dr. Scholl's Heel Cushions |
| Relatives: Billy Idol is his twin brother… | Description: Pale and pasty |

| Height: 6 feet | Family: Vampire | Habitat: Sunnydale, USA |
| Weight: 185 pounds | Origin: Unknown | Intelligence: |

THE MASTER

The Master is one of the founders of vampire society. He was trapped in The Hellmouth when he attempted to open it in order to unleash the demonic forces upon mankind. Now he must reside in The Hellmouth (an abandoned church where he held the failed ceremony) until he drinks the blood of a Slayer —like Buffy! His escape is referred to as The Harvest, a day when the blood of all mankind will flow. Has not been successful as of yet, though. Spends his days chatting with Quasimodo.

BEHAVIOR: Generally despicable and megalomaniacal. Seeks to bring about The Harvest at all costs.
LETHALITY: Very dangerous, paranoid, and unpredictable. Even kills his own kind.
WEAKNESSES: Has sense of humor (sort of), but no sense of style.
POWERS: All known vampire powers, plus black magic as well. He's a regular Bad News powerhouse. Can communicate with vampires sans phony Hungarian accent.

rotten teeth

henchmen

Height: 6 feet 2 inches	Family: Vampire	Habitat: Coffins made from palm trees
Weight: 225 pounds	Origin: Caribbean	Intelligence:

MAXIMILLION

Maximillion is the last of a race of Caribbean vampires, and he must find a new mate. Police detective Rita Veder had been chosen for the role due to her unknowingly being part vampire (on her father's side). Max journeyed all the way to Brooklyn to persuade her to fulfill her vampire destiny. But Rita had a boyfriend of her own and wasn't so easy to convince. After that thwarted romance, Max put out an ad in the personals of Vampire Weekly to find someone to sit with in front of a fire and walk with at midnight on the beach. His ad was answered by a lonely, middle-aged vampiress in Elyria, Ohio with big hips and a booty to match. Turned out, she was a vampire-making machine, and now Max isn't worried about his race dying out any time soon.

BEHAVIOR: Switches from Romanian-speaking Caribbean vampire to foul-mouthed ghetto thug at the drop of a bat's guano. Has a tendency to behave like a typical American-Italian male, doesn't think that romance or the woman's opinion matters.

LETHALITY: If his bite doesn't get you, his sense of humor will.

WEAKNESSES: Bad agent, bad hair, an adversity to sunlight and sharp wooden objects.

POWERS: While seeming to have all the usual traits of the vampire, he seems to have one over on Dracula. Most vampires breed by biting their victims and passing on the curse/power through the blood. Max has definitely kept his Mojo, as he seems to be able to mate by conventional human standards. But this ability seems to be all that Max has kept.

First Appearance: *Vampire in Brooklyn* (1995)	Endorsements: Little Richard's wavy hair gel
Relatives: Blacula	Description: Standup vampire

| Height: 6 feet 2 inches | Family: Vampire | Habitat: Old Castles |
| Weight: 160 pounds | Origin: Transylvania, Romania | Intelligence: |

NOSFERATU

Nosferatu – from the Greek meaning "plague carrier." The vampire plague comes to England in the form of Count Orlock. Real estate agent Knock sends his assistant Hutter to sell the Transylvanian nobleman a house. The Count lusts after Hutter's wife Ellen, who sacrifices herself to keep Orlock up after vampire-hours partying. The break of day leaves Nosferatu with more than a bad hangover…he seems to vaporize. But fear not—wherever girls are grinding to the beat, he's ready to help them into a state of oblivion.

ferocious buckteeth

BEHAVIOR: Lurking in shadows, sleeps all day, works all night, drinks only Type O blood.
LETHALITY: Bites cause vampirism, and overly histrionic contortions.
WEAKNESSES: Has mortal reaction to daylight, Bible thumpers, and Florence Stoker.
POWERS: Can levitate. Has a hypnotic stare and causes victim to become undead if bitten.

long, pointed nails

Nosferatu and Ellen Hutter

| First Appearance: *Nosferatu* (1922) | Endorsements: Marcel Marceau Mime School |
| Relatives: Wives rumored. | Description: Bald and uuugggly |

| Height: 5 feet 11 inches | Family: *Homo Sapien Electricus* | Habitat: American electrical grids |
| Weight: 180 pounds | Origin: State Prison, California | Intelligence: |

SHOCKER – HORACE PINKER

Electrocuted serial killer Horace Pinker gets his damned soul into the electric grid and uses it to travel about killing those who had put him in prison and testified against him. He tries real hard to be another Freddy Krueger, but doesn't quite make it. Still, be careful next time you plug in the hairdryer with the bathtub still full of water, because he just loves the smell of slightly singed hair.

BEHAVIOR: Supernatural stalking of his enemies via electrical devices and other anti-social, craven behavior.
LETHALITY: Very deadly electrical being.
WEAKNESSES: Hates damp places, those annoying plastic outlet covers, and grounded metal poles.
POWERS: Can migrate via electric wiring and possess people's bodies.

The birth of Shocker

| First Appearance: *Shocker* (1989) | Endorsements: General Electric Corp. of America |
| Relatives: Hannibal Lechter | Description: Ruddy complexion caused by electrocution |

Height: 4 feet	Family: Ghost	Habitat: Hotel buffets and hot dog stands
Weight: Weightless	Origin: Eastern Europe	Intelligence:

SLIMER

Believed to be the ghost of a cursed Lord from Romania who ignored the well-being of his subjects and dined while they begged for food. When a witch was put to the stake while he ate enough for six people, she cursed him to die and his ghost to be forever hungry. Although he can't stop eating, being a monster isn't so bad because you don't have to watch your cholesterol. He could be munching at a fast-food joint near you…

BEHAVIOR: Eats and eats and eats and eats.
LETHALITY: Only if you're between him and his next meal.
WEAKNESSES: His stomach.
POWERS: Can eat a lot. Passes through walls and people, leaves behind trail of ectoplasm or "slime." Causes people to lose their appetites for days.

stuffing his face

Slimer raiding dinner cart

green stomach

First Appearance: *Ghostbusters* (1984)	Endorsements: Weenies Wieners
Relatives: Casper	Description: Fat, green and slimy

Height: 5 feet 10 inches	Family: Vampire	Habitat: Sunnydale, USA
Weight: 170 pounds	Origin: London, England	Intelligence:

SPIKE

Spike was one of the worst Victorian poets. He liked womanizing and drinking and got zapped by vampire Drusilla, his ladylove then and now. This caused a lot of mixed emotions—just what a god-awful poet needs!!! He escaped his calling as a killer and hung with Buffy's gang until recently when he accidentally found salvation and is now human again and wants a more serious romance with Buffy.

bleach-haired bad boy

BEHAVIOR: Punkish attitudes. Very enamored of Buffy, still stinks as a poet and rebellious of modern society. Currently waiting for the phone to ring.
LETHALITY: Formerly had killer capability, but now only his poetry remains lethal.
WEAKNESSES: Over-estimates his creative abilities. Romantic to a fault.
POWERS: Great poser! Currently redeemed and human again. Formerly had all vampire advantages.

tough-guy leather jacket

First Appearance: "Buffy the Vampire Slayer" (1997)	Endorsements: FBI Records
Relatives: None known	Description: Pale pink skin, bleach blond hair, blue eyes

| Height: 5 feet 10 inches | Family: *Homo Lycanthropus Artificialus* | Habitat: Local small town high school |
| Weight: 160 pounds | Origin: California | Intelligence: |

TEENAGE WEREWOLF

Not a real werewolf, but a wolf-like creature generated by a serum developed by Dr. Alfred Brandon, a shrink who uses his troubled teenage patient Tony Rivers for unconventional hypnotic regression experiments. The transformation, like Jekyll to Hyde, became unstable and uncontrollable. NO Buddy Love here!!

BEHAVIOR: Howling, stalking of co-eds, destruction of school property, general juvenile delinquent antics.
LETHALITY: Can rip you up quickly. Has really bad dental problems and halitosis.
WEAKNESSES: No supernatural powers and is vulnerable to all weapons.
POWERS: Just a quick, agile killing machine with fur.

| First Appearance: *I was a Teenage Werewolf* (1957) | Endorsements: A.S.P.C.A. |
| Relatives: None | Description: Dark brown fur |

| Height: Various | Family: Vampires and shape-changers | Habitat: Caravans and castles |
| Weight: Various | Origin: Eastern Europe | Intelligence: |

VAMPIRE CIRCUS

Count Mitterhaus is a vampire that has been terrorizing this small quiet town for years. Finally the town's Mayor (or Burgermeister) has had enough when his wife succumbs to the charms and seductions of the villainous count. The villagers attack, killing Mitterhaus and destroying his castle. Fifteen years later, the town is ravaged by a plague. The only happiness they have known in months arrives in the form of a traveling troupe called Circus of Nights. Unbeknownst to the town folks, the troupe is led by Mitterhaus' brother, Emil, who wants to resurrect his brother using the blood of the women and children of the town. Alright! The circus is in town! Let's all go see the freaks!

BEHAVIOR: Most don't come out except at night, when all the circus performances are staged. They all seem friendly enough, but they are out to make Dracula look like a mosquito by comparison.
LETHALITY: Vampires, cat people and dwarfs combine to tear this village to pieces.
WEAKNESSES: Sun, stakes, and overconfidence.
POWERS: Flight, change into wolves, bats and panthers. All have long claws and/or sharp teeth.

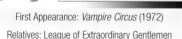
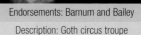

Height: 5 feet 6 inches	Family: Magic users	Habitat: Castles, schoolrooms
Weight: 120 pounds	Origin: Oz	Intelligence:

WICKED WITCH OF THE WEST

The Wicked Witch of the West is a fearsome force of hell—made from the stuff of nightmares. Not content to simply terrify residents throughout the kingdom of Oz, she often travels to our own world where she delights in creating mischief as a schoolteacher. Many of our readers most likely had her as a Math teacher when they were small and didn't realize their narrow escape in passing onto to the next grade. What other profession do you expect someone who plays with flying monkeys to have?

BEHAVIOR: This woman is on an eternal quest for power. The death of her own sister meant nothing to her except for the chance to steal the corpse's magic shoes. Her day is spent blending poisons and looking for people on whom she can try them out. Her nights are filled with nothing but murder and sarcasm.

LETHALITY: Extremely lethal. Not only is she willing to burn people alive with her own powers, she also commands a vast number of slave creatures. Ghosts, winged monkeys, lawyers and other heartless mutants make up her army of subordinates, all of who will kill for her without compunction.

WEAKNESSES: Falling houses, buckets of water, kindness

POWERS: Extensive: can command evil spirits, hurl fireballs, fly, levitate, spontaneously communicate, et cetera.

First Appearance: *Wizard of Oz* (1925)	Endorsements: Maxwell House Coffee
Relatives: Shannon Doherty, Wicked Witch of the East	Description: Broomstick wielding maniac

| Height: 5 feet 10 inches | Family: *Homo Lycanthropus* |
| Weight: 185 pounds | Origin: England |

WOLFMAN

Lawrence Talbot, son of Sir John Talbot, was bitten by a gypsy werewolf named Bela when the Romanian Gypsy clan passed through rural England. This bite caused a lycanthropic transformation during the full moon cycle and seriously cramped Talbot's social life. His mentor, the gypsy mystic Maleva was also the dead werewolf's mom and later leads him around Europe to find "peace" in death, cure or release from his Universal stock players' contract. The Wolfman has been known to wrestle Frankenstein's monster at charity events.

BEHAVIOR: Howls, stalks women, scratches fleas, rips up designer shirts, has aversion to fire hydrants and cats. He likes to vex doctors by telling them his life story. Usually committed to various loony bins to protect potential victims. Has been seen hanging with Abbott and Costello because The Three Stooges won't talk to him.

LETHALITY: Can tear your throat out, but most likely will bite you and turn you into a howling beast once a month.

WEAKNESSES: Hates silver bullets. If you sneak up on him and yell, "Hi yo Silver," he will soil himself. Also dislikes being clubbed with his own wolf's-head walking stick.

POWERS: Morphs from man to wolf in seconds during full moon. Mooning werewolves is not recommended.

First Appearance: *The Wolfman* (1941)

Relatives: Hugh Jackman

Habitat: London suburbs

Intelligence:

blood-stained teeth

hairy chest

Endorsements: Westminster Kennel Show

Description: Brown fur, sharp pointy teeth, underbite

MONSTERS FROM THE BEYOND

BEYOND: *That which is past or to a degree greater than knowledge or experience; the unknown; the world beyond death; the hereafter.*
          —The American Heritage Dictionary of the English Language

That is the dictionary's definition of the *Beyond*. Very fitting for the entries in this section, which feature monsters that are from a totally different realm never encountered before by humans. Friend or foe, there's no real way to tell as of yet. There is so much that we do not comprehend because we cannot pigeonhole it into the right mental compartment. We cannot ever fully understand what puts these dark forces to work and without that knowledge, we will always be left holding the empty box, and Pandora will always be regretting that she opened it.

And as we turn over new rocks, we always risk uncovering something that could be the end of us all. But should that stop our curiosity? Hell, no. It is our right to know who is sharing this universe with us. In reading this book and acting on what you have now discovered, you will be helping to turn the tide back for the good of all mankind (now go buy a copy for a friend).

| Height: 6 feet 4 inches | Family: Unknown | Habitat: Underground secret complexes |
| Weight: 240 pounds | Origin: Unknown | Intelligence: 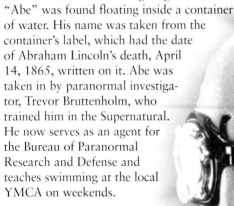 |

ABE SAPIEN

Abe Sapien was discovered when plumbers, working in the basement of Saint Trinian's Hospital in Washington, DC, broke open a sealed door and discovered a long-forgotten chamber. The creature called "Abe" was found floating inside a container of water. His name was taken from the container's label, which had the date of Abraham Lincoln's death, April 14, 1865, written on it. Abe was taken in by paranormal investigator, Trevor Bruttenholm, who trained him in the Supernatural. He now serves as an agent for the Bureau of Paranormal Research and Defense and teaches swimming at the local YMCA on weekends.

gotta keep those eyes moist

BEHAVIOR: Likes to read several books at once from the confines of his water tank, while eating rotten eggs (which he considers a delicacy).
LETHALITY: Abe is the sort of man-fish that would kill only in self-defense or as a last resort.
WEAKNESSES: A diet of rotten eggs makes keeping friends difficult.
POWERS: Psychic, aquatic abilities enable him to stay underwater indefinitely.

| First Appearance: *Hellboy* (2004) | Endorsements: Sea Monkeys |
| Relatives: Hellboy | Description: Greenish-blue goggled man |

| Height: 6 feet | Family: Scare fiend | Habitat: City Slums |
| Weight: 210 pounds | Origin: Chicago | Intelligence: |

CANDYMAN

There is a belief in the ghettos of Chicago of a man that is both protector and torturer. Here, no one dares say his name five times in front of the mirror. A university researcher named Helen investigates the local legend and discovers that Candyman is a ghost of an affluent slave. Tortured and murdered for making a white woman pregnant, he came back for revenge and has stayed ever since. He hangs out in seedy bathrooms, waiting for people to look in the mirror and beckon him. Better not play "Truth or Dare"...

BEHAVIOR: If you dare to say his name five times in the bathroom mirror he will appear and kill you. In Chicago at least, this proves to be true.

LETHALITY: Hook on his right hand where his original was cut off by the pregnant girl's father.

WEAKNESSES: His love for the girl.

POWERS: Nearly indestructible. Can appear where he wants and is not squeamish about killing women or harming small children and babies.

if you thought the hook was freaky, he wears this fur coat all year round

| First Appearance: *Candyman* (1992) | Endorsements: Captain Hook |
| Relatives: Cenobites; Night Breed | Description: Man in black fur coat |

| Height: 9 feet 8 inches | Family: Canine | Habitat: Hogwarts School of Wizardry |
| Weight: 670 pounds | Origin: Unknown | Intelligence: |

CEREBUS

Cerebus is the infamous three-headed dog that guards the entrance to Hell, entrusted with keeping the living from reclaiming the dead. He was fired because he was forever arguing with himself. These days, he guards the Sorcerer's Stone in the basement of Hogwarts School under the watchful eyes and control of Professor Albus Dumbledore, the school's headmaster. Now you know why the mail there is delivered by owls—and not mailmen.

BEHAVIOR: Will tear the head off anything that tries getting past him.
LETHALITY: Three large heads, three sets of big teeth, you do the math.
WEAKNESSES: Listening to music will put him to sleep, with the possible exception of Limp Bizkit.
POWERS: The dog is as big and bad as his bite.

while one head distracts you, the other attacks

no matter how often you clean it, it always has that wet-dank smell that is guaranteed to turn your stomach

doesn't want to mess up his hair

| First Appearance: *Jason and the Argonauts* (1963) | Endorsements: Animal Planet |
| Relatives: Scrappy Doo; Fluffy; Cujo | Description: Dog with three heads |

Height: 3 feet	Family: Humanoid	Habitat: Quiet Country Town
Weight: 60 pounds	Origin: England	Intelligence:

CHILDREN OF THE DAMNED

Spawned from every woman able to give birth in the small English village of Midwich after each had been in a deep, mysterious sleep. Each child has the same white hair and pale skin. They look eight years old, but are only two or three (they grew at an incredible, unnatural rate). They exhibit strange powers, revealing their malevolent natures. They are good at controlling parents and now propagate their evil through their very own cable company.

BEHAVIOR: Tendency to hang around in groups. All stop and stare at the same person at the same time. Don't like to be told what to do.
LETHALITY: Can make people kill themselves or fall off their bikes.
WEAKNESSES: Not fully grown yet, can still be fooled, just a little—just enough.
POWERS: Individually, they can make any adult do exactly what they want. As a group, nothing can stand in their way. Bright, glowing eyes, good for reading in the dark.

likes their clothes ironed and spotless

First Appearance: *Village of the Damned* (1960)	Endorsements: Trojan
Relatives: Lizzy Maguire and Amanda Bines	Description: Overgrown toddlers

| Height: 6 feet | Family: Scare fiend | Habitat: Fields and barns |
| Weight: 200 pounds | Origin: Midwest, USA | Intelligence: |

CREEPER

A terrible menace that feeds on people for their organs and covers his hideousness in a trench coat and floppy hat that hides most of his face. After leaving hundreds of his victims in a sewer behind an old church, he is discovered by siblings, who have a good chance of becoming his next meal. He was last seen raiding a roadside diner outside of Tuscaloosa where he was looking to feed on some portly truckers. If you see the Creeper hitching for a ride off of Route 1, keep driving.

Another of the "I'm so cool I can wear a trenchcoat in 100% heat" monsters

BEHAVIOR: The Creeper eats people to regenerate his own diseased body parts. He can actually see inside a person to see which body part, from which person, would suit him best. Drives around in a big black truck. Prepare to meet your Maker if passing through the Midwest you hear "Jeepers creepers" play on your radio.
LETHALITY: Almost impossible to stop without heavy hardware.
WEAKNESSES: Only able to feed for 23 days every 23 years.
POWERS: Nearly indestructible. Can absorb any body part from any human to add to his own disintegrating body. He can taste the fear in someone and track that person from miles away.

| First Appearance: *Jeepers Creepers* (2001) | Endorsements: Nachos |
| Relatives: Cenobites; Freddy Krueger | Description: Real-life scarecrow |

Height: 6 feet 2 inches	Family: Demigod	Habitat: Deathbeds
Weight: 210 pounds	Origin: Everywhere	Intelligence:

GRIM REAPER

The Grim Reaper resides in Hell, letting people know when their time has come to stop living. However, he becomes a pawn in a wicked, would-be dictator's plan for world domination to kill and replace two peace-loving rock gods, Bill S. Preston, Esq. and Ted "Theodore" Logan. Bill and Ted must outwit the Grim Reaper in order to get back to Earth. But Grim lets himself be outwitted by them because he thinks they're cool and becomes their friend. He gets them an audience with God, gets them back to school in time for the competition, and actually joins the band! After winning the Battle of the Bands, Grim goes back to his old job, because nothing is better than seeing the look on people's face when he turns up and points his bony finger at them. May be floating around a retirement community near you.

BEHAVIOR: Has no friends because they have all died on him. Social skills a problem, but he's trying.
LETHALITY: Just doing his job.
WEAKNESSES: Little or no sense of humor.
POWERS: He can be anywhere in the Universe where something is going to die. That means being in several hundred thousand places at once, all the time.

First Appearance: *Bill & Ted's Bogus Journey* (1991)	Endorsements: Ford, General Motors
Relatives: Little Nicky, Saddam Hussein	Description: Pale white face, dark hooded cloak

| Height: 2 feet | Family: Good Guys Doll | Habitat: Toy boxes |
| Weight: 10 pounds | Origin: Lake Shore | Intelligence: |

CHUCKY

Trapped by the police and fatally wounded, serial killer Charles Lee Ray uses a voodoo spell to transfer his soul into Chucky, a Good Guys doll. His hope is that when the time is right, he will be freed from the plastic prison by revealing his true identity to another human, which would trigger a soul switch between the two. He becomes the favorite toy of young Andy Barclay, who receives the Chucky doll as a birthday gift, and soon Charles Lee Ray resumes his killing spree. Hmm…a little doll that can kill. Seems like the perfect gift for that snotty kid down the street that always rings my doorbell and then runs away like it's funny to see someone open their door, look around, but not see anyone. That's it, you rotten kid! You've interrupted me during "Love Connection" for the last time!

BEHAVIOR: Pretends to be just a regular old plastic doll, then… STAB, you're dead. Oh, joy, what fun!
LETHALITY: How do you protect yourself from something like an innocent, sweet-looking toy?
WEAKNESSES: Doesn't like fire or extreme heat.
POWERS: Can turn his head and limbs all the way around.

the new "action man"

| First Appearance: *Child's Play* (1988) | Endorsements: Dolls of America |
| Relatives: Weird Al Yankovich | Description: Pink plastic |

Height: 2 feet	Family: Cranial nerves	Habitat: Glass bottles
Weight: 3 pounds	Origin: Germany	Intelligence:

BRIDE OF CHUCKY

Love is a strange thing. Plastic Chucky has a new girlfriend—a female doll, who happens to possess the soul of Charles' real-life girlfriend, Tiffany. But Tiffany has a mean streak of her own. And you thought "My Buddy" was creepy? Move over "Kid Sister." This femme fatale sports a leather jacket over her sequined wedding gown. Very classy.

move over joan rivers...

BEHAVIOR: Not a girl to trifle with. She wants a ring on her finger and she plans to have it. There is no "or else." Very knowledgeable in the occult and black magic, must have been what drew the two together in the first place.

LETHALITY: Her dress sense is almost as lethal as she is when she gets a knife in her hands.

WEAKNESSES: Finding makeup to cover burnt plastic.

POWERS: Can steal your body if she tells you her name, but prefers to carve her name on your open, bleeding heart.

First Appearance: *Bride of Chucky* (1998)	Endorsements: MTV and the Oscars pre-show
Relatives: Drew Barrymore	Description: Rose plastic

| Height: 5 feet 11 inches | Family: Bio-exorcist | Habitat: Graveyards and waiting rooms |
| Weight: 235 pounds | Origin: The Otherworld | Intelligence: |

BETELGEUSE

This self-proclaiming "Ghost with the Most" is a bio-exorcist. This means he helps ghosts get rid of living humans. Incredibly obnoxious and offensive, Betelgeuse is employed by Barbara and Adam Maitland, a couple recently killed in a car crash, to scare away the nasty humans, Charles and Delia Deitz, who have come to take residence in the Maitland's beautiful old farmhouse. But the Deitz' daughter, Lydia, can see through all of Betelgeuse' tricks. Nowadays, Betelgeuse can be found coasting the malls with Lydia—the two have become almost inseparable. They even starred in a TV show together.

BEHAVIOR: Annoying extrovert. He loves an audience ("ShowTime!" is his catchphrase). Lies, cheats, and would sell his soul (if he had one) for fast cash.
LETHALITY: He'll scare you to death (if his body odor doesn't get you first).
WEAKNESSES: He can't go anywhere unless someone calls his name three times (Candyman beware!).
POWERS: Can make his body into anything he chooses, even a carousel.

used car salesman's smile

used car salesman

flares are back in style

| Height: 25 feet 10 inches | Family: Titan | Habitat: Remote Greek islands |
| Weight: 890 pounds | Origin: Unknown part of the Universe | Intelligence: |

CYCLOPS

*the ultimate
"uni-brow"*

The Cyclops lives alone on an isolated Greek island and raises goats and sheep for food (although he has been known to nibble on the occasional lost sailor). Sinbad encountered the Cyclops on his Seventh Voyage and whacked the big boy in the eye with a sharp stick, which proves that you can learn valuable lessons from reading the classics in school. Would love to find a nice pair of sunglasses that actually fit his eye, since, as of late, he's been sporting one pathetic eye patch.

BEHAVIOR: Herding, roaring, marauding unwanted Greek visitors and throwing huge boulders at various military targets.
LETHALITY: Can bash in your brains and rip men limb from limb. Cyclops is the model for most modern-day nightclub bouncers.
WEAKNESSES: Monocular vision, no depth perception. Clumsy, slow movements.
POWERS: Brute Strength

| First Appearance: *The Seventh Voyage of Sinbad* (1958) | Endorsements: Governor of California |
| Relatives: Cyclops (of the X-Men) | Description: Hairy freak with one eye |

| Height: 6 feet 2 inches | Family: Scare fiend | Habitat: Dreams |
| Weight: 250 pounds | Origin: Elm Street | Intelligence: |

FREDDY KRUGER

The teenagers of Springwood all have something in common—their nightmares. They are all dreaming of the same grotesque man, his face melted and disfigured, knives on every finger of his right hand…Freddy Kruger is his name and killing these kids is going to be his game. Freddy is the spirit of a child killer in Springwood, who was beaten and burnt alive by the townsfolk. Like any good villain, Freddy comes back to haunt their kids. The scarier he becomes, the more they fear him, and the more they fear him, the stronger he grows. Eventually he has enough power to kill them in their dreams. Works long hours during TV marathons of "My Favorite Martian."

extra crispy skin

please do not try this at home

BEHAVIOR: Loves to tear people apart as gruesomely as possible, but only after scaring them to the brink of death. He enjoys watching the suffering he causes and the fear he creates. Pulled wings off insects and played with his food as a child.
LETHALITY: If you fall asleep and he's there, there is a 99 percent chance that you'll die.
WEAKNESSES: Lack of fear and bravery in victim. Needs people to believe in him to survive.
POWERS: Can kill you in your sleep. Knows your worst fear.

sweater from mom (explains everything)

| First Appearance: *Nightmare on Elm Street* (1984) | Endorsements: D.A.R.E. |
| Relatives: Jason Vorhees; Michael Myers | Description: Melted skin, knives for fingers |

Height: 2 feet 6 inches	Family: *Mogwai Hairus*	Habitat: Warm, dark bedrooms
Weight: 50 pounds	Origin: The Orient	Intelligence: 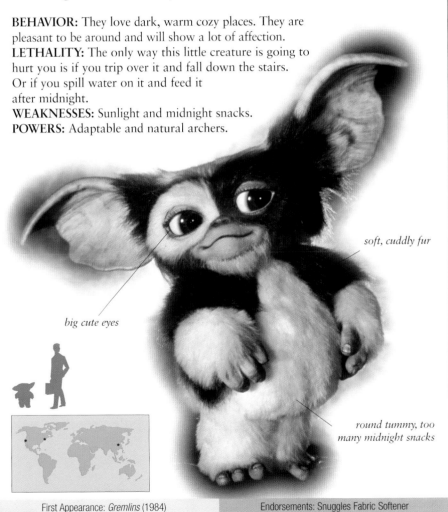

GIZMO

A Mogwai who is bought by a middle-aged inventor named Rand Peltzer for his son comes with three warnings: (1) Keep away from bright lights. (2) Never give water. (3) Never, ever feed after midnight. What? C'mon—why wouldn't you give your pet any water? Who knew that the cute little fur ball would turn into a creature from Hell from a slice of pizza in the middle of the night? I've heard of heartburn, but this is ridiculous. Next time you see a random Mogwai being sold in the streets of Chinatown, just keep walking. Oh, and grab me some Kung Pao chicken while you're there.

BEHAVIOR: They love dark, warm cozy places. They are pleasant to be around and will show a lot of affection.
LETHALITY: The only way this little creature is going to hurt you is if you trip over it and fall down the stairs. Or if you spill water on it and feed it after midnight.
WEAKNESSES: Sunlight and midnight snacks.
POWERS: Adaptable and natural archers.

soft, cuddly fur

big cute eyes

round tummy, too many midnight snacks

First Appearance: *Gremlins* (1984)	Endorsements: Snuggles Fabric Softener
Relatives: E.T.	Description: Chinese Care Bear

| Height: 2 feet 6 inches | Family: *Mogwai Deformus* | Habitat: Anywhere |
| Weight: 50 pounds | Origin: The Orient | Intelligence: |

GREMLIN

When the rules of looking after a Mogwai are broken, look out! Billy hasn't listened to his dad and feeds the young Mogwai after midnight. This causes extreme pain for the young creature that culminates with eggs popping off its body. These eggs hatch into Gremlins. The Gremlins first nearly destroy Billy's hometown of Kingston Falls, and then, years later, they reappear in New York to reek destruction on a cable TV network.

BEHAVIOR: They avoid sunlight, which is no great loss to them, as they are totally nighttime party animals. They love a good drink and a great time out, especially if it is at someone else's expense. While the majority just love to party, some have mutated with greater degrees of personality and intellect.

LETHALITY: Just hope they don't find a microwave oven in your size. And keep away from water at all costs.

WEAKNESSES: Sunlight and electricity.

POWERS: Strong and adaptable little creatures.

very popular fashion statement among monsters

loves to entertain his victims

| First Appearance: *Gremlins* (1984) | Endorsements: Hershey's Chocolate |
| Relatives: Stripe, Brain, and Sean Penn | Description: Lizard-skinned demon |

Height: 4 feet	Family: *Harpis Aviarius Bitchy*	Habitat: Colchis
Weight: 100 pounds	Origin: Mediterranean regions	Intelligence:

HARPIES

The Harpies are the daughters of the giant Thaumus and the nymph Elektra. They have female heads and breasts, but eagle bodies. They were once described as beautiful winged women, but later emerged as hideous old hags with crooked, razor-sharp talons. The Harpies guard the Golden Fleece, which is hidden in the ruins of Colchis.

BEHAVIOR: Fly around and deface Greek palaces, and other former ancient hot spots, similar to pigeons in Central Park. No statue, Greek or otherwise, is safe. They like ruining major explorations, and buffet picnics. These noisy, filthy creatures are used by the Gods to punish criminals. They often torment the insane. They are not to be confused with HARPOS, an altogether different type of insanity.

LETHALITY: Can squawk you to death like your Aunt Frances. Not lethal, but after a while you'll wish you were dead.

WEAKNESSES: They are always hungry and must eat constantly. Harpies hate loud music and being beaten with sticks by Greek heroes.

POWERS: Harpies can fly, are very maneuverable and possess a loud ear-piercing screech. They have impenetrable, armored feathers.

large leather wings capable of a top speed of 300 mph while carrying two people

shows off by crushing skulls with them at parties

believe me, you don't want to know

Height: 6 feet 4 inches	Family: Marine	Habitat: The ocean floor, bargain bins
Weight: 245 pounds	Origin: The briny deep	Intelligence:

HUMANOIDS FROM THE DEEP

For some unknown reason, mutant salmon take on humanoid form and then come ashore to find beautiful human women with whom to mate. Clumsy and stupid, they are easily repelled by everyone from small children to grandmothers. They have not been seen since their first foray into the world of surface dwellers.

mutant head drooping with slime

BEHAVIOR: Not very predictable. These creatures stumble about looking for women, or simply letting their curiosity get the better of them, much like members of high-school science clubs.
LETHALITY: Not very lethal. Although fearsome-looking, these creatures are very much like their salmon ancestors, and don't seem nearly as inclined to murder as they are to mating.
WEAKNESSES: Soft heads, slow movements, bad writers.
POWERS: Able to breathe underwater and swim with some speed.

First Appearance: *Humanoids from the Deep* (1980)	Endorsements: Red Lobster
Relatives: All they can spawn	Description: Green, slimy seafood

Height: 6 feet 5 inches	Family: *Halloweenus Sapien*	Habitat: Nightmares and spooky stories
Weight: 180 pounds	Origin: Halloween Town	Intelligence:

JACK SKELLINGTON

When Jack Skellington, the Pumpkin King of Halloween Town, grows bored of trying to scare the same old people each and every day with the same old tricks and treats, he looks around for something new. He tries to take over Christmas, but fails miserably because he ain't no Santa Claus. Red isn't his color anyway. Lately, he can be found back on the Halloween scene, scaring trick-or-treaters.

BEHAVIOR: Wickedly cruel and armed with a twisted sense of humor, he will do anything to anyone to get a scream or howl, even if it means taking his own head off.

LETHALITY: Not much chance of him killing anyone, unless it's with a heart attack. He prefers to scar people emotionally rather than physically.

WEAKNESSES: Just doesn't understand anything but Halloween.

POWERS: With every scary monster and creature that has crawled around under every bed at his disposal, he is the king of soiled bed sheets.

voted sharpest dresser on E! fashion awards

First Appearance: *The Nightmare Before Christmas* (1993)	Endorsements: American Dental Association
Relatives: Michael Moore	Description: White stick figure

Height: 5 feet 2 inches	Family: Mutated Human	Habitat: Suburbs of Los Angeles
Weight: 137 pounds	Origin: Africa	Intelligence:

LEECH WOMAN

An aging, rich, spoiled, and neglected housewife named June Talbot accompanies her doctor husband to Africa, where an old man has promised to reveal the secret of a root powder that will arrest the aging process in humans. June learns the process of how the fluid from the pineal gland of a freshly killed man, when mixed with the powder, restores her youth and beauty. Her husband happens to be the fresh meat used by the old man in his demonstration. Suddenly single and armed with a supply of the powder, June—now a gorgeous femme fatale—returns to the USA only to find that she has to keep killing guys to get the pineal fluid or she turns back into an old bag. Not the worst way to spend your life.

BEHAVIOR: Primping and preening, strangling and shooting boyfriends. The Leech Woman is definitely a one-night stand.
LETHALITY: As lethal as ladies can get. Don't turn your back on this one.
WEAKNESSES: Vanity, thy name is woman.
POWERS: No special powers, just instinct to stay young and pretty forever—just like Cher!!!!

this is what happens if you don't use sunblock

she killed everything herself

First Appearance: *The Leech Woman* (1960)	Endorsements: Wrinkle Cream
Relatives: None	Description: Wrinkled rich lady

Height: 5 feet 3 inches	Family: Demigoddess (Mortal)	Habitat: Private Mediterranean Island
Weight: 130 pounds	Origin: Greece	Intelligence:

MEDUSA

Medusa is the mortal daughter of Ceto and Phorcys (her sisters, Stheino and Euryale, are both immortals). Medusa was beautiful and vain. But when she rivaled Athena for the favors of Perseus, she was turned into a snake-haired monster that can change people into stone by looking at them. Supposedly her blood is toxic too, so don't go sinking your teeth into her neck anytime soon.

snakes by Versace

BEHAVIOR: Medusa is looking for the right guy, but keeps meeting losers and ambitious adventurers who think she is a "mere female." They soon find out how wrong they are when they become stone art pieces for her garden.
LETHALITY: Direct eye contact causes petrifaction, even after her decapitation.
WEAKNESSES: Vanity (there are no mirrors in her palace). She has a heart of glass and a short-fused temper. Snakes in hair tends to turn off suitors.
POWERS: Her stare can cause living beings, mostly unfaithful men, to turn to stone. Her blood can heal the sick and raise the dead.

First Appearance: *Jason and the Argonauts* (1963)	Endorsements: www.venomousreptiles.org
Relatives: Hydra; Gorgon	Description: Snake-haired serpent woman

| Height: 5 feet 10 inches | Family: Human | Habitat: Pyramids and Museums |
| Weight: 180 pounds | Origin: Egypt | Intelligence: |

THE MUMMY

Naughty High Priest gets caught with his pants down with the Pharaoh's wife. Gets his tongue cut out, major organs removed and embalmed, all while still alive. Buried with his extended family and friends. Curse and spells enable him to come back to life in order to find the resurrected woman he loved, rule the world, and live happily ever after killing millions of people.

tight lipped because they cut out his tongue

four miles of wrapping makes it hell when you need a bathroom

BEHAVIOR: Can't keep his hands to himself or find his own girlfriend. Wraps himself up as a present, then buries himself for a few thousand years. Sucks the flesh off of others to replace his own.

LETHALITY: Not only can he control evil little bugs that can eat you in seconds, he loves doing it, and will probably be only too happy to do it to millions of us if he ever takes control of the world.

WEAKNESSES: Falling in love with the wrong women, forever losing spell books.

POWERS: Brute force, can control the elements, controls flesh-eating scarab bugs, able to open mouth really, really, wide.

| First Appearance: *The Mummy* (1932) | Endorsements: Band-Aid |
| Relatives: George Hamilton | Description: Man wrapped in gauze |

Height: 6 feet 3 inches	Family: Demon	Habitat: Leviathan
Weight: 210 pounds	Origin: England	Intelligence: 

PINHEAD

During the First World War, Captain Elliot Spencer bears witness to so many atrocities that he actually develops an appetite for pain and torture. After the war, he travels to the Middle East and discovers the Lament Configuration— a small puzzle box that when solved, opens the mystical doorway to a hellish realm of pain and torture known as Leviathan. Elliot is sucked through and initiated into the order of the gash, a society of pain beyond limits. Leviathan is now his domain. Now with his crown of golden pins deeply embedded into his skull, Pinhead walks the corridors of Hell commanding its insane nightmares and horrific denizens, waiting to torture any living fools rash enough to open the Lament Configuration.

gold pins driven into his brain

sidelines as a dentist

BEHAVIOR: Totally insane and sadistic.
LETHALITY: Spins long chains around his body that can skin a man in seconds, while keeping them alive, of course.
WEAKNESSES: Movies with happy endings. Smart Alecs that can withstand pain and solve puzzles. Junior Mints.
POWERS: Bullets or conventional weapons have no effect. Can rip the flesh off your bones, instill the darkest fears deep in your soul and love every minute of it.

First Appearance: *Hellraiser* (1987)	Endorsements: Flying Fingers Knitting shop
Relatives: Conehead	Description: Human pin cushion

Height: 30 stories	Family: Confectionary	Habitat: Gateways to other dimensions
Weight: 2000 tons	Origin: Sumeria	Intelligence:

STAY-PUFT MARSHMALLOW MAN

This roly-poly confection, known as the Stay-Puft Marshmallow, is the creation of the evil demigod Gozer who wants to destroy mankind. Gozer was kind enough to offer the paranormal investigating team, Ghostbusters, the chance to choose the form in which he would wipe out mankind (he's real sadistic like that!). All they have to do is think it, and it would be created. Dr. Raymond Stanz tries to imagine the one thing that he feels could never hurt them—the big blob of marshmallow known as "Stay-Puft Marshmallow Man." But this giant cream puff can do a lot of damage. Think of a 2000-ton baby who hasn't had his nap. Not a pretty sight, but awfully cute though. Having fallen on some hard times, Stay-Puft currently scrapes out a living appearing in commercials for tires and cookie dough.

BEHAVIOR: Hides in refrigerators, possesses people, and transforms them into horrific Terror Dogs.
LETHALITY: Out to destroy all mankind and has the chops to do it.
WEAKNESSES: Melts in contact with proton weapons. Boy scout troops and law suits from parents of fat kids.
POWERS: To crush and smother all those in its path. Diabetics beware.

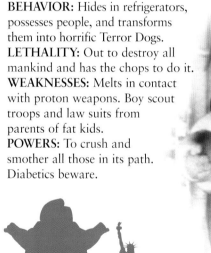

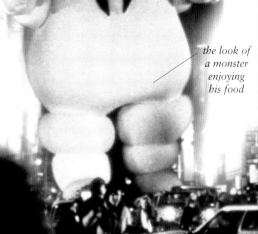

the look of a monster enjoying his work

the look of a monster enjoying his food

First Appearance: *Ghostbusters* (1984)	Endorsements: Rice Krispie treats
Relatives: Pillsbury Doughboy	Description: White cream puff

| Height: 6 feet 2 inches | Family: Magic users | Habitat: Castles, museums, paintings |
| Weight: 220 pounds | Origin: Eastern Europe | Intelligence: |

VEGO

Cursed and trapped within a living painting for all time, this cruel and wicked dictator languished in captivity for several centuries. Eventually he was removed from the castle where he had been locked away, and he was transported to NYC. There, he influenced a weak-minded curator and escaped his prison—albeit only temporarily. Currently hanging out in the Louvre, he's back in his frame. When not having relations with Mona Lisa, he's slowing down tourist lines and knocking off museum guards who fall asleep while on duty.

BEHAVIOR: When not gazing out from a two-dimensional perspective, this supreme egocentric lives a completely hedonistic lifestyle, existing only for the moment. His appetites large, his demands insane, and his patience nonexistent, this is one being to be avoided at all costs.

LETHALITY: Hostile to the max. Will murder any who displease him. Will break the legs of a baby just for laughs.

WEAKNESSES: Supremely powerful in his day, he is confounded by some inventions of the modern world. Can battle all forms of magic and physical attack, but would probably fall for a whoopie cushion.

POWERS: Unlimited magical abilities.

| First Appearance: *Ghostbusters II* (1989) | Endorsements: David Copperfield |
| Relatives: The Picture of Dorian Gray | Description: Angry old man in golden armor |

MONSTER SIZE COMPARISON CHART

Just for the hell of it, we'd thought you like to see some of these monsters stacked up against one another to see whom the real big boys are.

Killer Ants • Savage Bees • Piranhas • Hitler's Brain • Gizmo • Tiffany • Chucky • Flying Monkeys

Slimer • Harpies • Killer Tomatoes • Wicked Witch of the West • Nosferatu • Jack Skellington • Hounds of the Baskervilles • Hellboy • Frankenstein's Monster

Beast of Hollow Mountain • Anaconda • King Kong • 50-foot Woman • Tarantula • Gorgo

4'
3'
2'
1'

Feathered
Hen

Cujo

Gremlin

Children of
the Damned

Slimer

20'
18'
16'
14'
12'
10'
8'
6'
4'
2'

Big Foot

Cerebus

Hydra

Beast of Hollow
Mountain

200'
180'
160'
140'
120'
100'
80'
60'
40'
20'

Beast from
20,000 Fathoms

Rodan

Godzilla

Deadly Mantis

Mothra

500'

450'

400'

350'

300'

250'

200'

150'

100'

50'

The Statue of Liberty
(For Size)

Stay-Puft Marshmallow Man

HOW TO PROTECT YOURSELF AGAINST MONSTERS

Just a cursory glance over the "Checklist" on the proceeding pages, and it is immediately clear that the number of Monsters is pretty daunting. You cannot expect to be fully prepared and armed at all times, should you be suddenly attacked by one or more of these Monsters. Arming yourself with knowledge about these monsters can be your greatest weapon. We can't stress enough the importance of using this Field Guide. Even in his smaller, more modest edition, Professor Van Helsing knew that properly used, THIS BOOK CAN SAVE YOUR LIFE.

First, there are those items you can easily carry around in your pocket book, jacket or on your person.

THE CRUCIFIX: Universal symbol of Good. This will ward off most vampires, as will the Star of David, or any other major religious icons. Our advice is to always wear it around your neck. It may be in easy reach of a breast pocket or handbag, but vampires rarely come at you with warning. This way, if they try to bite you, they'll suddenly be thrown back by the power of the symbol around your neck.

If this happens, the vampire will stagger back in pain and shock. Get away as fast as you can without looking back. Do not try pressing towards the vampire with the cross. This is a typical beginner's mistake. No, after his initial shock, he will focus on you instead. If you make eye contact with the beast, you're a goner. It will hypnotize you into throwing the cross to one side and then kill you on the spot.

SMALL GARLIC SPRAY (TO BE CARRIED IN YOUR POCKET): It's like the old pepper spray cans, but with garlic solution instead. This sprayed directly into a vampire's face will blind him for days and may even permanently scar him.

SILVER BULLETS: If you're intending on carrying a gun, make like the Lone Ranger and use silver bullets. The Lone Ranger carried them for a reason. The silver bullet will stop not only vampires, but werewolves as well. The silver spreads out on impact, tearing their hearts to ribbons. Just be careful, as the older the vampire, the more explosive his end can be. Such combustion's will leave terrible burns on the carpet.

RUNNING SHOES: The "must-have" item is a good pair of running shoes because even in your dreams, when the bogiemen come, you have got to get running.

Obviously, to battle all the monsters featured in this book would mean you would have to carry everything from missile launchers to cans of Raid on your person at all times. This would be a problem for most, but there are solutions. As we said earlier, consult your guide as you move about. Have with you what is recommended for specific areas. In the workplace, for instance, pool resources with your co-workers and have a few essentials at the office. Let your employer know that the government now offers tax breaks for having full monster-fighting defense plans and weapons in the workplace.

Be extra careful at home with this equipment, especially if there are children around. Don't ever let the kids know where the weapons are as children are usually the first to be turned by an invading force. Don't give evil an advantage.

And as a final note (we can't emphasize this enough): MEN BEWARE. Despite what you see in the movies, men are more frequent victims than women are. When stalking her prey, a female vampire does not have to wait for her victim to be alone. Any time is an opportune time. All she has to do is flirt a little with the guy, toss back her hair and give him a playful smile, and the poor fool is hooked. Before he knows what hits him, he's vampire food.

CHECKLIST

- ☐ Alligator
- ☐ Anaconda
- ☐ Beast of Hollow Mountain
- ☐ Beast from 20,000 Fathoms
- ☐ Crab Monsters
- ☐ Creature from the Black Lagoon
- ☐ Crocodile
- ☐ Gorgo
- ☐ Dragons
- ☐ Godzilla
- ☐ Gwangi Dinosaurs
- ☐ Hydra
- ☐ Jaws
- ☐ The Loch Ness Monster
- ☐ Orca
- ☐ Piranhas
- ☐ Q
- ☐ Reptile
- ☐ Rodan
- ☐ Squid
- ☐ Tyrannosaurus Rex
- ☐ Amazing Colossal Man
- ☐ Giant Ant
- ☐ Killer Ant

- ☐ Ape
- ☐ Dr. Zaius
- ☐ Beast
- ☐ Big Foot
- ☐ Black Scorpion
- ☐ Cujo
- ☐ Deadly Mantis
- ☐ Eight-Legged Freaks
- ☐ The Fly
- ☐ Brundlefly
- ☐ Flying Monkeys
- ☐ Freaks
- ☐ Frogs
- ☐ Gorgon
- ☐ Hound of the Baskervilles
- ☐ Hulk
- ☐ Invisible Man
- ☐ Jason Voorhees
- ☐ King Kong
- ☐ Michael Myers
- ☐ Mighty Joe Young
- ☐ Minotaur
- ☐ Morlocks
- ☐ Mothra

- [ ] Professor Alberto Levin
- [ ] Quasimodo
- [ ] Savage Bees
- [ ] Sasquatch
- [ ] Scorpion King
- [ ] Shrek
- [ ] 50-foot Woman
- [ ] Tarantula
- [ ] The Thing
- [ ] The Incredible Melting Man
- [ ] The Incredible Shrinking Man
- [ ] Wasp Woman
- [ ] Audrey II
- [ ] Killer Tomatoes
- [ ] Pods
- [ ] Swamp Thing
- [ ] Triffids
- [ ] Jack Torrance
- [ ] Mr. Glass
- [ ] Dr. Caligari
- [ ] Dr. Cyclops
- [ ] Dr. Victor Frankenstein
- [ ] Dr. Jekyll/Mr. Hyde
- [ ] Dr. Moreau
- [ ] Hannibal Lechter

- [ ] Son of Frankenstein
- [ ] Jack the Ripper
- [ ] Joker
- [ ] Leatherface
- [ ] Norman Bates
- [ ] Phantom of the Opera
- [ ] Bride of Frankenstein
- [ ] Colossus
- [ ] Frankenstein's Monster
- [ ] Hal 9000
- [ ] Edward Scissorhands
- [ ] Maria the Robot
- [ ] RoboCop
- [ ] Mechagodzilla
- [ ] Replicants
- [ ] Hitler's Brain
- [ ] Frankenstein's Teenage Monster
- [ ] Terminator
- [ ] Gunslinger
- [ ] Angel
- [ ] The Crow
- [ ] Blacula
- [ ] Blade
- [ ] Christine
- [ ] Count Downe

- ☐ Count Vlad Dracula
- ☐ Dracula's daughter
- ☐ Golden Vampire
- ☐ Golem
- ☐ Grandpa Munster
- ☐ Hellboy
- ☐ Lestat de Lioncourt
- ☐ Little Vampire
- ☐ Living Dead
- ☐ Lost Boys
- ☐ The Master
- ☐ Maximillion
- ☐ Nosferatu
- ☐ Shocker-Horace Pinker
- ☐ Slimer
- ☐ Spike
- ☐ Teenage Werewolf
- ☐ Vampire Circus
- ☐ Wicked Witch of the West
- ☐ Wolfman
- ☐ Zombie
- ☐ Abe Sapien
- ☐ Candyman
- ☐ Cerebus
- ☐ Children of the Damned

- ☐ Creeper
- ☐ Grim Reaper
- ☐ Chucky
- ☐ Bride of Chucky
- ☐ Beetlegeuse
- ☐ Cyclops
- ☐ Freddy Kruger
- ☐ Gizmo
- ☐ Gremlin
- ☐ Harpies
- ☐ Humanoids from the Deep
- ☐ Jack Skellington
- ☐ Leech Woman
- ☐ Medusa
- ☐ The Mummy
- ☐ Pinhead
- ☐ Stay-Puft Marshmallow Man
- ☐ Vego

ABOUT THE AUTHORS

Abraham Van Helsing was very progressive with his approach to science. He traveled the world, giving various lectures in both anthropology and philosophy (secular and religious), and he taught at the major universities of the world, such as the University of Leyden, Trinity College, and Oxford University. But his new calling was the study of vampirism. At first he doubted its existence until his inheritance of property in Rumania brought him face to face with the infamous Count Dracula, who was then the cult leader of the Children of Judas. Van Helsing made the mistake of underestimating the dark powers of the cult, and this mistake cost his wife, Elizabeth, her life. He dedicated the rest of his life to ridding the world of the curse of Dracula and the disease of vampirism.

The original version of this book is Van Helsing's only published work.

Dave Elliot has worked in every aspect of comic and magazine publishing from paste-up artists and art director; through to writer and publisher, earning himself several awards from all over the world. Up until recently he was the Humor editor for *Penthouse* magazine and he took the leap from frying pan to the fire by entering the film industry. He optioned his first script, then a second, and is now doing project development work for some major Hollywood producers. Dave hasn't left the comic industry behind. He operates a boutique publishing company with his partners at Atomeka Press, and recently wrote *Bible Eden*, an illustrated adaptation of the story of Adam and Eve. He currently enjoys the relative peace of living in Small Town, USA where he can enjoy watching his daughters (Crazy) Amy and (Loopy) Lizzy grow up.

C.J. Henderson has, in his time, earned his keep as a: movie house manager, waiter, drama coach, fast-food jockey, interior painter, blackjack dealer, book reviewer, stockman, English teacher, roadie, advertising salesman, creative writing instructor, supernatural investigator, bank guard, storage coordinator, children's theater director, card shark, film critic, dishwasher, magazine editor, traffic manager, short-order cook, stand-up comic, interview & general article writer; toy salesman, camp counselor, movie booker, street mime, lounge lizard, and a senior editor of legal publications. These days, C.J. is married to fashion designer Grace Tin Lo. They live in Brooklyn, NY, with their daughter Erica, a noisy bird, Mr. Exciting, and two cats, Tyco and Tiger.

R. Allen Leider is best known as feature writer and reviewer for the now defunct *Monster Times* fan newspaper and for the original story and screenplay for "The Oracle" (1985). He has been a working film critic since 1970, including a three year stint on WWFM radio with his own "Cinemascene" program. He is publisher and critic for *The Black Cat Review* online magazine. For ten years, he was EVP of Donna Gould Public Relations and now works as a freelance PR, marketing, and media consultant. He lives in New York City with his wife and four feline Egyptian gods.

PHOTOGRAPHY CREDITS

All photographs courtesy of the Kobal Collection.

20th Century Fox: 3, 13, 22, 46, 49, 53, 60, 61, 107, 119
20th Century Fox Television: 147
7 Arts: 41, 157
AIP: 8, 13, 16, 48, 64, 85, 104, 125, 132, 153
Alan Lansburg/ Don Kirshner: 79
Alcor: 13
Alive: 150
Allied Artists: 13, 26, 82, 92, 93, 95
Amblin: 45, 55
American Zoetrope: 13, 16, 164
Amicus: 17
Burton: 175
Canal Plus: 13
Carolco: 126
CBS: 54, 141
Cinemarque-Film Futures: 158, 179
Columbia: 13, 20, 23, 68, 69, 102, 128, 134, 136, 142, 151, 160, 169, 173, 180, 181
Columbia Tri-Star: 32, 33
Cometstone: 144
DC Comics: 108
Decla-Bioscop: 100
Deutsche Bioscop: 140
Di Novi: 175
Dimension Films: 129
Disney: 12, 30, 31, 52
Dreamworks: 76
Electric Entertainment: 13, 59
Falcon International: 71
Famous Film Productions: 39
Fox 2000: 29
Gaumont: 149
Geffen: 13, 143, 158, 168
Hammer: 6, 8, 13, 18, 41, 49, 65, 102, 136, 137, 139, 154, 156, 157
HBO: 82
Image Ten: 145
King Brothers: 34
LADD Company: 112, 123
Larco: 40
Leone: 77
Light Year: 88
Magnum Pictures: 71
Marvel: 13, 47, 66
MCA: 141

MGM: 13, 62, 63, 74, 103, 105, 113, 118, 127, 155, 162, 177
MGM British: 163
Miramax: 129, 131
Morningside: 35
Nelson Entertainment: 165
New Amsterdam: 13
New Line: 1, 14, 31, 133, 144, 170
New World: 28, 158, 174, 179
Orion: 13, 105, 121, 165
Paramount: 12, 13, 31, 16, 30, 31, 51, 70, 97, 101, 103, 110, 117, 148
Piranha Productions: 28
Polygram: 161
Prana-Film: 149
Pressman/Most: 131
Propaganda: 144
Regency: 13
Revolution: 13, 128, 142, 160
RKO: 5, 72, 73, 78
Santa Cruz: 87
Santa Rosa: 125
Shaw: 139
Sony Pictures: 68
Strike Entertainment: 13
Swamp Films: 94
Taft Entertainment: 57
TOHO: 13, 15, 17, 32, 33, 42, 43, 75, 122
Touchstone: 99, 175
Tri-Star: 13, 128, 142, 160
U.S. War Department: 124
UFA: 120
UNI: 84, 86
United Artists: 24, 38, 80, 93, 166
United Film: 14, 145
Universal: 6, 12, 13, 15, 18, 21, 27, 30, 37, 45, 47, 55, 58, 66, 67, 81, 83, 102, 105, 106, 111, 114, 115, 116, 135, 137, 138, 141, 150, 153, 167, 176, 178
Village Road Show: 13, 59
Vortex: 96, 109
Walt Disney Pictures: 15, 44, 46
Warner Bros.: 13, 14, 25, 50, 56, 89, 90, 98, 108, 112, 123, 146, 158, 168, 171, 172
WB TV: 82, 130